NATIONAL INSTITUTE SOCIAL SERVICES LIBRARY
NO. 34

STAFF AND STUDENT SUPERVISION

National Institute Social Services Library

STAFF AND STUDENT SUPERVISION

A Task-centred Approach

DOROTHY E. PETTES

London
GEORGE ALLEN & UNWIN
Boston   Sydney

First published in 1979

STAFF AND STUDENT SUPERVISION A Task-centred Approach *replaces* SUPERVISION IN SOCIAL WORK A Method of Student Training and Staff Development which was first published in 1967, fourth impression 1973.

GEORGE ALLEN & UNWIN LTD
40 Museum Street, London WC1A 1LU

© George Allen & Unwin (Publishers) Ltd, 1979

British Library Cataloguing in Publication Data

Pettes, Dorothy Elizabeth
   Staff and student supervision. – (National Institute
   for Social Work. Social Services library; No. 34)
   1. Supervision of social workers
   I. Title   II. Series
   658.3'02   HV41   78–40856

   ISBN 0–04–361033–1
   ISBN 0–04–361034–X   Pbk

Typeset in 10 on 11 point Times by Northampton Phototypesetters
and printed in Great Britain
by Hollen Street Press Ltd, Slough

CONTENTS

Preface

PREFACE

In the decade since I wrote *Supervision in Social Work* many significant changes have occured in social work. It follows that expectations of supervision have been affected by these changes and supervisors face new demands and the challenge of developing new skills in supervision.

In this book I have endeavoured to discuss some of these new demands and to suggest ways in which supervisors may meet them. Perhaps the two most significant changes have been reflected by the increasing need for staff supervision and the ever widening demands on supervisors as skill and knowledge grow in so many varied methods of social work. Both these developments pose some difficulties in organising a book on supervision. What should one discuss as basic to all social work supervision? What is special to staff or student supervision? Should supervision in community work be discussed separately from supervision in casework or residential work or group work? Must each separate section repeat what is basic to others? I could find no 'ideal' answers to these questions. The structure for which I settled will be apparent in the table of contents.

I do believe that most of the important elements in the role of a supervisor in social work remain constant whatever method is practised or whether the supervision is related to staff or students. I have tried to show the common basic elements in Chapter 1 and to recognise what is different in supervision in the various methods of social work practice in Chapter 2. In the separate sections on staff and student supervision which form the major part of this book most of the discussion will apply to all methods. Where there are differences for a particular method, I have described them. I have also drawn illustrations of supervisory practice from a variety of methods. Any reader wishing to follow in sequence all references to a particular method may use the index to locate material throughout the book.

I have listed references and suggestions for further reading at the end of each chapter. I have usually only mentioned a book or article once, placing it after that chapter for which it seemed most appropriate. However, it should be apparent that the books on staff supervision by Kadushin and Westheimer relate to all of the chapters in Part Two, while those by Kent and Young on student supervision relate to the chapters in Part Three.

A further decision a writer must make is with regard to the use of personal pronouns. For the sake of consistency I have in most cases used the masculine, but obviously it represents both sexes throughout.

PREFACE

Although as a social work educator, I have needed to be familiar with developments in a variety of social work methods, my own early orientation was in the casework method. I am indebted to Nan Bridgeford, Haydn Davies Jones, Madeline Malherbe and Dorothy Stock Whitaker for helping me to understand more of the methods in which they have expert knowledge. I am also greatly indebted to E. Matilda Goldberg and to Olive Stevenson for their separate and generous responses to my inquiries regarding their researches into the social work task. Most of all I am grateful to Marie Ellert who has patiently read the manuscript of this book and whose criticisms, suggestions and support have been invaluable. Finally I must pay tribute to Mrs Vera Ford who has dealt so competently and efficiently with my chaotic typing and American spelling.

PART ONE:
INTRODUCTION TO SUPERVISION IN SOCIAL WORK

Chapter 1

---◆---

ROLE AND FUNCTION IN SUPERVISION

This book is about the process of supervision in social work generally. From this base it will examine the various aspects of supervision and explore how a task-centred approach may aid the supervisor in providing a flexible yet purposeful form of supervision that may meet the worker's or student's needs and enhance the service to clients. Supervisors have needs, too. They need, above all, to feel satisfaction in a job well done. It is hoped that the methods of supervision discussed here may suggest some ways of meeting that need.

DEFINITION OF SUPERVISION

What is Supervision?
Supervision is a process by which one social work practitioner enables another social work practitioner *who is accountable to him* to practise to the best of his ability. Social workers frequently ask each other for support or advice, but in doing this they are not asking for supervision. Almost all social workers are accountable to someone else for the work they do. Accountability does imply some sense of supervision. Someone may be looking at one's work, yet this reviewing need not necessarily be accompanied by any responsibility for helping the worker to improve his practice. Over the years, social workers have developed a concept of supervision which has seen the supervisor as responsible not only for holding the worker accountable for doing his work but enabling and, if necessary, teaching him so that he may do his work well. This joining of responsibilities has not been accepted without question. Attempts have been made through the years to divorce the administrative and teaching functions, perhaps the most successful currently being in Switzerland.[1] However, for most supervisors the demand remains that they shall help someone, either student or worker, who is accountable to them, to practise to the best of his ability. A task-centred approach to supervision has as its goal providing a framework for the practice of supervision that is precise, so that the supervisor may know specifically what he is doing, and goal oriented so that the supervision may be purposeful. This approach may be used effectively

in both student and staff supervision and for supervising in all methods of social work. It involves maximum participation between supervisor and supervisee because both must understand and agree the goals and tasks undertaken.

Let us, however, return to the definition and examine some of the implications. 'Supervision is a process . . .' We speak of the casework process or the process of any other method. We use process recording to describe the series of interactions and interventions in which a social worker may engage to attempt desired ends. Hopefully these interactions and interventions are planned and purposeful although also arising out of both intuitive and trained responses of the social worker. So it is with supervision. Supervision may be described as one of the many methods or processes of social work. To describe supervision thus should help us to a clarity of purpose and method that will avoid the old fear of supervision as an attempt to 'casework the caseworker'. For all social workers, including supervisors, an ultimate goal must be to help the client; but unlike those social workers who work directly with clients, the supervisor's immediate task is to help the worker achieve this end. The skills involved are the same as in other methods of social work but, focused on a different goal, they produce a method in which both 'caseworking the caseworker' and 'group-working the team' are inappropriate.

In the definition used, the reference is to 'one social work practitioner' helping another who is accountable to him. The person designated supervisor is a social worker and will use social work skills and knowledge. He or she may be a caseworker, a group worker, a community worker, or a practitioner of any other method that may be covered by the generic term social worker. Whatever his frame of reference, the fact of accountability is an essential one. The person becoming a supervisor has taken on responsibility for assuring that work is done, that either worker or student achieves that which it has been agreed should be accomplished. So the worker or student is accountable to him; and the supervisor, knowing the quality of the work done, has a responsibility to use his skills to enable the practitioner to develop his practice to his maximum capacity.

Knowledge and Skills Needed

The knowledge and skills needed for supervision are basically the same as those on which the supervisor will have relied as a social worker. After all we have just defined supervision as a process or method of social work, and the supervisor will be dealing with social workers and social work problems. However, the way in which he uses his knowledge is different, and the skills upon which he calls must meet rather different demands. Skills must be further developed in some areas rather than others.

All social workers should have some knowledge and skill in administration. The social worker's service to his clients will be better if he knows his way around the agency, knows how to use policies and procedures for the benefit of his clients rather than finding himself constantly frustrated or hindered because he has not gone through appropriate channels. When that social worker becomes a supervisor, he will find himself needing more and more to develop his skills in administration. Now if he chooses the wrong procedure more people may be hampered or frustrated. He is there to see that his workers are freed to do their jobs, not to hamper them because no answer has been received from an urgent but wrongly addressed memo. He will find himself needing thoroughly to understand policies because he will need to interpret them to others. He must understand them, too, in order to assess the implications for workers and clients so that he can give warning if the policies may have negative effects on the work. He will find himself dealing with masses of paper work – reading records, memos, reports for a variety of reasons. He will be filling out forms and asking his workers to fill out forms – to what end? He must understand the reasons for the variety of paper work if he is to cope effectively. He must be able to organise his own work and help his workers organise theirs. He must make decisions about everything from whom to alert on a case of suspected battering to how many forms will be needed to carry out a survey. Most certainly he will need to develop his administrative skills. If constant exercise has anything to do with it, they will develop rapidly.

Teaching skills are also important to a supervisor. If he is to help a variety of workers perform to the best of their capabilities, he will inevitably be involved in teaching much of the time. Sometimes all that is needed is information giving. At other times the learning/teaching process will involve a complex programme of the use of various teaching devices for both individuals and groups. Helping a worker or student to gain new knowledge may involve different processes from those involved in helping him to learn skills in practice or to change attitudes. The supervisor will draw on all that he has learned about teaching methods and all that he knows of what makes people learn. His own experiences of learning will influence his perception of what he will need to do as a teacher. His knowledge of human behaviour and of motivation will help. With all of this as a base, he will probably find that he still wishes to widen his knowledge further and develop skills in a variety of ways of teaching as he proceeds with his supervisory tasks in this area.

Many writers add a third skill, that of enabling. It is a skill that is involved in both administration and teaching. It has sometimes been described as providing a climate in which the practitioner can use supervision. Others have described it as a constellation of the supportive elements in supervision. It has much to do with the kind of relationship which is developed between the supervisor and worker or student. Social workers who become supervisors have generally developed considerable skill in building relationships and are aware of the factors that affect relationships. This is a colleague, not a client, relationship; but it is still a professional relationship. Supervisor and supervisee have been brought together for a purpose, and each has a role to play. For the supervisor, it is important that he conducts himself in such a fashion that the worker may learn to trust him. He must be aware of the worker's needs in relation to the job and offer appropriate support when it is needed. 'Support' can cover such varied activities as backing a worker's decision, providing precious time by helping a worker organise his work, or providing a sympathetic ear when the inevitable emotional demands of the work press heavily. The skill of enabling is involved in building differential relationships which will allow each individual worker or student to function well with the supervisor in both the administrative and learning aspects of their shared tasks. It takes skill, indeed, to provide such a differential approach which is yet fair and consistent and seen to be so.

Skills in communication interweave with all three skills mentioned so far. Without skill in communication administration becomes chaotic, teaching is confused, and enabling is impossible. Most social workers have of necessity developed considerable skill in communication. The supervisor may find, however, that he needs to broaden his skills in both verbal and non-verbal communications. An awareness of what his team is really communicating to him by repeated absences from meetings will be important. So, too, will be his ability to digest complicated or specialised documents and to translate them into comprehensible terms. His mid-position between workers and management make it essential that he be able to communicate clearly and quickly both orally and in writing.

Finally, the supervisor will use all of the knowledge of social work he may have gained through education and experience. He may not use the knowledge now in direct work with clients, but in the course of time the problems his workers face and discuss with him may call on any part of it. This knowledge may be used in teaching and problem-solving discussions, but it must be applied differentially to the new situation. It is not usually helpful to say, 'I had a case like that and I did . . .'. Even in the remote event of the cases' being identical, the worker is a different person bringing different skills and abilities to the situation. The supervisor should share his knowledge and experience with the worker, but he will need to recognise that they may be applied differently.

Variations in Supervision

What has been said about supervision so far, the process, the skills and knowledge needed, can be applied in any field of social work. There are variations in application in different disciplines, and they will be discussed in the next chapter. In all methods the supervisor does engage in a social work process; he does use skills in administration, teaching, enabling and communication; and he does draw on his knowledge of social work. Obviously a supervisor of caseworkers will draw largely on his knowledge of casework although hopefully he will have further generic knowledge as well. The community worker will draw on his knowledge of community work and find all his skills in working with individuals and groups involved as well as in his practice of supervision. The same holds true for the group worker or the residential worker.

All of the knowledge and skills described thus far may be used by the supervisor in either individual or group supervision. If the supervisor has more than one worker or student, he will be involved in at least some aspects of group supervision. Traditionally emphasis has been placed on one-to-one aspects of supervision, but increasingly today the values of group supervision are becoming recognised. Most supervisors of teams now use both methods to complement each other and meet different needs. The process of both individual and group supervision will be discussed in subsequent chapters as will aspects of peer group supervision.

THE SUPERVISOR WITHIN THE AGENCY

The Organisational Base of Social Work

It may be said that the supervisor is an organisational man. The whole concept of his mid-position seems to rest on an assumption of organisational hierarchy. While many social workers protest against organisational restraints, the fact remains that social work has been and continues to be almost universally based in organisations. A few social workers may perform some forms of social service individually as in private practice, but the vast majority of social workers and clients are dependent upon organisations to bring them together and to provide the means of helping. Like it or not, most social workers are dependent upon organisations for an opportunity to do the work they have chosen.

A fact of life for most social workers is that they are more apt to be working in a large and complex organisation today than they might have been ten or twenty years ago. Populations increase, needs increase, and social work organisations grow larger. In Britain we have seen larger units of organisation following each of the reorganisations of the local authority social services. Recent reorganisation of the probation service has left most probation officers working in larger units. The national voluntary organisations have had to devise new structures to meet the needs of changing patterns of service delivery throughout the country.

All of this has on the one hand exacerbated the need for understanding organisational matters and on the other frequently increased the feeling of the basic grade social worker of distance from the decision-making centres of power. How may he hope to influence policy if he is only one of several hundred workers? What notice will be taken of his client's need no matter how eloquently he may word his memo, if that memo is likely to be blocked at any one of several levels before it reaches the eyes for which it was intended? The medical social worker, used to working in a host agency, may have difficulty explaining to an area director, used to working in a primary agency, just why a certain policy will upset the doctors and thus impair rather than facilitate the social services to patients. A community worker outposted in a neighbourhood centre may find himself dependent for resources on a central office director who has little knowledge of the methods he uses.

Equally top administration may feel cut off from the actual provision of services. It is their responsibility to provide the machinery for meeting client need, yet the very complexity of the machinery may make it difficult to know or understand how the work is being done.

The Supervisor's Linking Role
Because of this increasing distance, the role of the supervisor or team leader has become crucial, for he is the vital link in connecting management with the operational level. In social work agencies the product is a service to clients; the goals are related to providing timely specified services to clients as efficiently and effectively as possible. So it is the basic grade social workers – those who work directly with clients be it individually, in groups or in the community sphere – who are at the operational level, the level that produces the services by which the agency may be judged. All other positions (including the supervisor's) are supportive rather than operational. The typist supports the operational work. The training officer supports the operational level. So does the person who may co-ordinate the work. So does the director who provides structures and policies designed to make the operational work possible. In fact all activity of a social work organisation is geared to producing the requisite service at the operational level.

The position of the supervisor in the organisational hierarchy is the administrative post closest to the operational level. He provides the key link between management and operational levels; and because it is a crucial linking role, the demands are for knowledge and skill in both management and practice. He must understand management roles and aims. He must see himself as a part of the management team with all the responsibility this implies for assuring effective service at the operational level. To assure that service he must also thoroughly understand practice roles and aims. He must see himself as a social work practitioner with all the responsibility this implies for professional standards, ethics and concern for the client. To meet this dual demand is not easy. Considerable space in subsequent chapters will be devoted to looking at how it may be done.

Organisational Accountability and Professional Responsibility

For many workers and supervisors one of the most difficult questions to answer has been whether or not the worker's accountability to a supervisor detracts from his own professional responsibility. Comparisons have been made with the medical and legal professions where it is said any decision based upon a professional judgement may only be called in question by the professional bodies concerned. This is not true to date for social workers. Not only is social work generally practised from an organisational base, but throughout its history much of the work has been done by professionally unqualified workers. At the time of writing, at least, it is clear that the professional associations for social workers do not have the same power of sanctions as those in the medical and legal professions to maintain standards.

In an organisation there must be some accountability. In a social work organisation the end product, the service to clients, will depend in the long run on a multiplicity of professional judgements about how and when that service should be offered. Social workers in such organisations usually come with a variety of backgrounds and qualifications for making such judgements. Where, then, can professional responsibility fairly lie?

There are no easy answers to this question. Social workers have still to work out exactly what they mean by 'professional responsibility'. Probably most would agree that if a worker was asked to do something that violated the code of ethics published by his professional association, this would require a refusal on the grounds of professional responsibility. Professional judgement, however, is not so clear cut. Professional opinion may differ as to the correct assessment of a situation or what interventions are appropriate. Who is equipped to make professional judgements? We may say that all professionally qualified workers must take professional responsibility on the basis of their judgement. What, then, of the mature social worker who happens not to have a qualification but brings a high degree of skill and years of experience to bear in making his judgement? Should not his professional responsibility be recognised? On the other hand the fact that someone is in a post designated 'social worker' does not necessarily mean that he is able to take full responsibility for using professional judgement when he has no experience or training to equip him to do so.

However difficult it may be to define, all members of a profession or even a semi-profession do carry a sense of professional responsibility which they cannot abdicate whether working alone or in an organisation. This holds true for both worker and supervisor. In a situation where the demands of an organisation appear to conflict with demands of professional judgement each must make his own judgement and be prepared to take whatever consequences ensue.

In the day-to-day functioning of an agency, however, there is but rarely a dramatic conflict over professional responsibility. A variety of workers with a variety of capabilities are required to make a variety of professional decisions,. some of them of life or death importance as in the case of suspected non-accidental injuries. For the most part they make these decisions with the help and support of their supervisors. How much help is offered, how much authority is exerted, may well depend in the main on the judgement of the supervisor. If the worker is very new and brings to his post no experience and no training, it would be unfair to hold him responsible for decisions he is not equipped to make. The supervisor must help him to assess the factors and in some instances may even firmly over-rule his judgement. The situation is very different with a fully qualified, professionally able worker. In many important decisions such a worker will welcome consultation with his senior colleague and make use of his advice in coming to his decision. It is in those rare instances when an impasse is reached, the supervisor advocating one course of action and the worker determined on another, that the question of professional responsibility arises. There is rarely only one answer in social work, and the supervisor may well decide that, having warned the worker of his doubt regarding the proposed course, there is nothing for it but to see what occurs with whatever result being, indeed, the worker's responsibility. However, the supervisor, too, has a professional responsibility and an agency responsibility; and if he has reason to believe that either the client will be seriously damaged or the agency brought into disrepute, he must take the matter further. Usually he will seek consultation, and often the worker will join him in seeking another opinion. After all neither worker nor supervisor wishes damage to occur; the difference is in the assessment of risk that it will. However, in most social agencies there is a point at which the worker's individual judgement may be over-ruled.

There may be differences of opinion as to whether this is desirable or not, but it is a fact of life for most social workers. In so far as it puts the client's interests above considerations of professional status or pride it may certainly be defended. Many workers are glad of shared responsibility. Others, reasonably secure in their own competence, want the right of consultation but would prefer to accept sole responsibility for the final decision. So long as we have staffs of mixed abilities, training and experience in social service agencies, the degree of responsibility that can be left to an individual worker must vary.

TASK-CENTRED SUPERVISION

The Need for a Task-Oriented Approach

Thus far we have been considering what supervision is, the knowledge and skills required and how the supervisor functions in a profession whose work is organisationally based in agencies. Before beginning the detailed analysis (in the chapters that follow) of how a supervisor works, it is necessary to explain the frame of reference of a task-centred approach.

Interest in a task-centred approach to social work has been stimulated by a number of factors. The phrase itself, now so popular, probably stems from William Reid's writings about casework;[2] but the concept relates far more broadly than to casework alone. The need for more purposeful work, for delineation of tasks and activities to be accomplished in relation to goals, for agreement between clients and workers, has long been recognised by all methods of social work. Hey and Rowbottom point to the similarity to management by objectives and go on to develop their own well delineated concept of tasks in relation to social work practice and supervision.[3]

The need to be precise about what we are doing has never been more apparent. During the twentieth century social work has been a growth industry as more and more social needs have been identified. In the early part of the century this growth was manifested in the increasing number of agencies. Recently in Great Britain many of these agencies have been consolidated into fewer but larger agencies. The number of social workers employed and the money spent on social services has grown enormously in the first three-quarters of the century. Such obvious expenditure demands accountability. The public rightly wants to know what it is getting for its money. All too often the accounting has been vague. We have had difficulty spelling out what we are attempting to do and hence difficulty in measuring the success or failure of our efforts.

At the same time we are feeling the pressure of more and more demands on our services. If we are to work effectively, we must know what we can do and what we cannot do. If priorities must be set, if choice must be made, again we must know with much more precision than in the past what the tasks are, how long it takes to achieve them, always in relation to what we are trying to do and how effective are the methods we use.

Fortunately all these pressures have stimulated research which may help us with the answers. At the time of writing Stevenson is nearing completion of a three-year project reviewing social workers' tasks.[4] Goldberg is testing a case review system to provide basic information about social workers' activities and their effect on client systems.[5] Rowbottom and others have published a study of work patterns and organisation in social service departments and are continuing research in this area.[6] The British Association of Social Workers has published a comprehensive report of its working party on the social work task.[7] In countless social service departments and other social agencies, smaller studies are being carried out aimed at identifying tasks and goals for social work.

Definition of Task

Already sufficient has been published to help the supervisor use a task-oriented approach in his work. Task has been defined as 'a specific piece of work with an end point, which requires a comprehensible programme of activity in order to attain it, and which has in it implicitly, if not explicitly, a time scale'.[8] 'Task' is a rather more precise description of activity than 'duty'. Two supervisors may each have the general duty of evaluating the work of members of their team. One may fulfil his duty by keeping a general eye on the work during the period to be evaluated (say six months) and at the end of the time writing down his impressions and submitting the evaluation to the proper source. The other may make careful notes after each supervisory session. He may discuss with the worker his impressions after three months, pointing up areas in which the worker is doing particularly well or in which she will need to bring her work up to standard before the six-month evaluation. He may agree a specific programme of activity required by both worker and supervisor to enable the worker to progress. Two weeks before the evaluation is due, he may set aside time to review a sample of the worker's cases and then have an evaluation session with her before he writes the evaluation. He then writes it, shares it with the worker, and finally turns it in to the proper administrative officer. Both supervisors have discharged their duty to evaluate a worker. One has designed a comparatively simple series of tasks; the other, a complex programme of activity. If we think only in terms of what duties the supervisor has to fulfil, we will have little idea how much time and effort will be involved. By looking at the tasks each has set himself, we have a much more explicit idea of the work involved.

So a task is specific. It has an end point, a goal to be reached. In the illustration above the specific end point was to evaluate the worker and a date was set explicitly at the end of six months. The goal most certainly governs the type of work, the programme of activity, to be specified. As the illustration shows, the task can be perceived differently by different people. Similarly a worker's tasks and duties may be differentiated. Two probation officers may each have the duty of seeing a boy on probation for regular reporting sessions. One may fulfil his duty by seeing him at specific intervals for a friendly chat with nothing planned ahead as to content. The other may use the sessions for a highly sophisticated type of play therapy. The duty is the same; the task description very different. Both tasks may be entirely appropriate. The needs of the particular boy may have been in the one case for friendly chats, in the other for play therapy. It is up to the worker to assess not only what the boy needs but what he, the worker, has the skill to offer.

In both illustrations there happens to have been an automatic time limit set, one by the evaluation date, the other by the probation order. For most social work tasks no such precise time limit is set automatically, and it is part of the skill of designing tasks to be able to recognise the implicit if not explicit time limit. A worker may set himself the task of helping a mother to gain more understanding of her son's emotional needs, or a supervisor may set himself the task of helping one of his workers improve her recording. In each case a programme of activity will be devised aimed at achieving a goal. It will be important to spell out what will constitute evidence that the goal has been achieved. How much understanding is needed? What standard of recording is to be achieved? As we look at the tasks and look at the goal, we must surely have an approximate idea of how long this ought to take. If this estimated time is included in the task definition, it gives a point for assessment. Has the task been accomplished, the goal reached? If not it is time for review and a decision as to next steps, very possibly a redesigning of tasks, perhaps even a shift in goals.

A task, then, is at once varied and precise. It can be designed to describe an infinite variety of social work activity, but the description itself is extremely precise, embodying as it does a fully worked out programme of activity directed toward a specific goal to be accomplished within a recognised time scale. Such a concept is not without its critics. There are those who think task-centred work may develop too rigid adherence to what may appear to be mechanistic routines. Certainly no one would advocate an approach which eliminates spontaneity of thinking and feeling or creative activity in response to the immediate situation. Such difficulty need not occur if the concept is applied flexibly and imaginatively. No one expects that every social work transaction will be programmed or that interactions between person and person or person and groups of persons can be subject to rigidly planned formulae. The fact that individuals are involved with their many and varied responses and investments in the outcome is a protection against the routinised process that some fear. As with the application of all concepts in social work, the human element will dominate the system.

The Supervisor's Use of a Task-Oriented Approach

A supervisor can make use of a task-oriented approach in many ways. In the first place he can use it for himself. That is, as he looks at his duties and responsibilities, he breaks them down into tasks to be accomplished. Much of the rest of this book will be devoted to discussing factors he will need to take into account when planning programmes of supervisory activity. Such an approach helps the supervisor to clarify his role, to understand exactly what he is doing, and to set priorities for himself and his workers or students. It helps in sorting out what should be done and what can be done. It is a valuable tool for self-assessment in that it provides frequent opportunities for review as the supervisor assesses his completion of each task.

The task-oriented concept is of great use in relation to workers or students as well. Knowledge of their work is essential to the supervisor, and a recognition of the tasks involved gives a clear picture. Helping the worker to formulate his work in terms of tasks makes for a more planned and purposeful approach on his part. It also helps the supervisor to understand the exact nature of the work load, and he can gear further assignments accordingly. He may vaguely know that one worker has a number of complex cases and another is carrying a rather more routine caseload, but if he knows the precisely worked out tasks of each, he is in a much better position to allocate work fairly.

As we shall see in Parts Two and Three, perhaps most importantly of all, a task-oriented approach helps in providing flexible supervision to meet the needs of workers or students with varying degrees of knowledge and skill. For the inexperienced, the supervisor may take a leading role in working out tasks with the worker, helping him to undertake work appropriate to his abilities. With more experienced workers or students, the supervisor may well play a more consultative role, helping where necessary or where 'two heads are better than one' to work out the goals and strategies. Very able and experienced workers, used to working independently, may rarely need any help in working out their tasks, but may use this as a way of maintaining their accountability to the supervisor. By informing him of the tasks undertaken, they give him a clear account of the sort of work they are doing, and together the supervisor and worker may review at given intervals to see how the tasks have been accomplished. This is not to say that because a goal has not been reached there will be a negative evaluation. They may agree that both failed to recognise certain elements that made the task impossible or that unforeseen events negated the work, but the information is there for mutual assessment of the work.

Finally, the very specificity of a task-oriented approach makes it a good source for identifying needs that cannot be met through lack of resources, skills or time.

CONCLUSION

We have seen in this chapter that supervision is a process which may be practised by social workers and which involves specific skills and knowledge. Supervision may be said to be an organisational concept, and the supervisor's position of accountability and responsibility within the hierarchy shapes the concept of his role. A task-centred approach to supervision which is both precise and goal oriented helps the supervisor to encourage planned, purposeful work; and it helps to make accountability clear.

REFERENCES

1 See the February 1976 issue of *Sozialarbeit Travail Social*, magazine of the Association of Swiss Social Workers. The issue is devoted to Supervision; see particularly articles by Doris Zeller and Helen Eier (in German with French résumés).
2 William Reid and Anne Shyne, *Brief and Extended Casework*, Columbia University Press (1969); William Reid and Laura Epstein, *Task-Centred Casework*, Columbia University Press (1972).
3 Anthea Hey and Ralph Rowbottom, 'Task and Supervision in Area Social Work', *The British Journal of Social Work*, vol. 1, no. 4 (1971).
4 Olive Stevenson, 'Focus on the Task of the Local Authority Social Worker', *Social Work Today*, vol. 9, no. 4 (1977).
5 E. M. Goldberg and David Truin, 'Towards Accountability in Social Work', *The British Journal of Social Work*, vol. 6, no. 1 (1976).
6 Ralph Rowbottom, Anthea Hey and David Billis, *Social Service Departments*, Heinemann (1974).
7 BASW Working Party, Janie Thomas, Chairperson, *The Social Work Task*, Trafford Press (1977).
8 Hey and Rowbottom, op. cit.

FURTHER READING

Andrew Billingsley, 'Bureaucratic and Professional Orientation Patterns in Social Casework', *Social Service Review*, vol. 38, no. 4 (1964).
Ann Glampson and E. M. Goldberg, 'Post-Seebohm Social Services: (2) The Consumer's Viewpoint', *Social Work Today*, vol. 8, no. 6 (1976).
Richard Hall, 'Professionalization and Bureaucratization', *American Sociological Review*, vol. 33, no. 1 (1968).
Archie Hanlon, 'Casework Beyond Bureaucracy', *Social Casework*, vol. 52, no. 4 (1971).
Jean Hardy, 'The Knowledge Base of Professionalism with Particular Reference to Social Work', *Social Work* (British), vol. 27, no. 2 (1970).
Gordon Laurence, 'Organizational Choice as an Issue', *Social Work Today*, vol. 4, no. 8 (1973).

June E. Neill, R. William Warburton and Brendon McGuinness, 'Post-Seebohm Social Services: (1) The Social Worker's Viewpoint', *Social Work Today*, vol. 8, no. 5 (1976).

Alwyn Roberts, 'Boundaries of Professional Autonomy', *Social Work Today*, vol. 5, no. 8 (1974).

Brian Roycroft, Elizabeth Birchall and Jack Rothman, 'Post-Seebohm Social Services: Reactions to the Studies', *Social Work Today*, vol. 8, no. 7 (1976).

Harry Wasserman, 'The Professional Social Worker in a Bureaucracy', *Social Work* (U.S.), vol. 16, no. 1 (1971).

Chapter 2

———◆———

SUPERVISION IN SPECIALISED FIELDS

Concepts of supervision have developed along with other concepts of social work practice from an ever expanding knowledge base. If we are to see how these have been affected by new developments through the years, we must start with the origins in casework before looking at supervision in other methods.

EARLY DEVELOPMENTS IN CASEWORK

Historical Development

The development of supervisory practice in social work dates back to the beginnings of casework. The first function to be recognised as necessary was administrative. Naturally when more than one social worker worked in an agency someone had to organise the work. Someone had to make assignments. Someone had to see that the work was done. With the establishment early in the twentieth century of training for social workers at the London School of Economics in Britain and Columbia University in the United States, it became apparent that social work was at last starting to develop as a profession. From the first, social work educators recognised the importance of field training and sought to place their students with experienced workers. It was a time of experimentation as students and supervisors and workers and supervisors learned together. Knowledge that was being taught on courses had come from the field and needed to be continually retested in the field. Educators were excited by the theories of John Dewey. Learning by rote was discarded for learning by doing. Obviously the field work supervisor had an important part to play. Thus the caseworkers (for they were largely concerned with individuals and families) started on the long road to formulating concepts of supervision which would make a constructive contribution to their practice.

Not unnaturally the caseworkers relied on the skills they had developed in practice, and so supervision was individually focused. The helping and teaching roles soon overtook the administrative. As Freudian interpretation of behaviour influenced casework theory, they also permeated theories of supervision. This led to a focus that often seemed to concentrate more on the worker or student than on the work to be done. Resistance must be interpreted and transference handled. Out of this sort of supervision came legitimate fears that supervisors were 'caseworking the caseworker'. At the same time supervisors were also assimilating ideas from non-directive therapy, and 'What do you think?' became an overworked phrase in supervision. It is a sound educational dictum that a student should be encouraged to think for himself, but it can be and sometimes was carried to extremes.

However, as time passed concepts of supervisory practice changed with experience. In part this may have reflected changes in casework practice as the sometimes over-enthusiastic commitment to Freudian ideas was modified. It was also the result of pragmatic assessment of what worked and what didn't. A tripartite concept of supervision was conceived by Towle which included administrative, teaching and enabling functions.[1] The emphasis shifted more to the work and away from the personality of the worker. Because the worker must use himself skilfully and with self-awareness in his work with clients, there remained an area in which it could still be legitimate to discuss personal matters so long as they appeared to affect the work.

As has been noted earlier, it has not been easy to maintain a balance of functions. At different times and in different places either the administrative or the teaching and enabling functions have been in the ascendant. In the fifties Austin and others called for separation.[2] Although many attempts have been made, complete separation has rarely been achieved. It appears an inescapable fact that administrative decisions do affect professional decisions and set the boundaries in which they may be made. Currently agencies in Switzerland have developed a practice of dual supervision. The worker is administratively accountable to one person in his agency but is supervised professionally by another whose services may be purchased from outside the agency.[3] Early reports indicate considerable satisfaction with this system although it is not quite clear whether the 'outside supervisor' has the authority of a supervisor or acts more in a consultant capacity. For the most part in the United States and Great Britain supervisors, both staff and student, continue to carry responsibility in both areas. One or the other may be seen as of paramount importance, or there may simply be a blending. This depends in part on the desires of the supervisor and in part on the organisational structure in which he works.

Characteristics of Supervision Peculiar to Casework
For the most part the supervisory concepts that were developed when casework was the major method of practice hold good for other methods as well. However, certain characteristics seem peculiarly related to the casework method.

By the nature of casework practice, supervisors in this method have limited opportunities to observe their students or workers in action. A supervisor can, of course, arrange to participate in a joint interview with a worker, but it rarely occurs out of a natural need for two workers in the situation. In group work, community work and residential work there are rather more opportunities for joint work in the normal course of the day. The casework supervisor has had to concentrate on ways of helping his supervisee to present at second hand a clear picture of what has happened. Because the account must be filtered through the perception of the worker, it is important to get it in some detail and as soon as possible before significant factors are forgotten. This obviously affects the style of recording required, the frequency of supervisory sessions, and the content of those sessions. In recent years we have learned that it is possible to introduce another participant, an observer, a tape-recorder or even all the equipment for video-taping into the one-to-one interview without damage in selected situations. A casework supervisor may arrange to supplement the student's reporting in such fashion, and for educational or training purposes this has proved a useful tool. However, the fact remains that for day-to-day purposes such artificial arrangements seem rather impracticable.

Casework is also differentiated from other methods by the numbers involved, and this brings both problems and advantages. The sheer volume of workers and clients means that for the most part the work is performed in large hierarchically structured agencies. The worker or student is far removed from the director and top management. This makes heavy demands on the supervisor in his linking role, and the supervisee may feel unsure as to his recourse should the supervisor fail him in some way. On the other hand, the large number of clients is an advantage, particularly to a student supervisor who may the more precisely select a caseload geared to an individual student's needs.

GROUP WORK AND COMMUNITY WORK

Common Factors in Newly Developing Fields

As we saw with casework, there are problems in developing supervision when fields of practice are themselves in a developing stage. Although both group work and community work have been practised for some years, they are still relatively recent compared with casework; and as a result they are experiencing some of the problems seen in the early days of casework. Inevitably the role of the supervisor is not as clearly defined, and there is usually a shortage of supervisors trained in the method to be practised. As we saw with casework, in the early days it is often a question of workers and supervisors learning together, experimenting together in developing the new method. This is often an exciting and satisfying period. There may, however, be some unease in working out relationships where one of the innovators has been assigned a position of greater authority or accountability than the other. Eventually a stage is reached where there are some workers trained in the new method or with more experience than others who can bring to their positions the authority of knowledge as well as of position. In the interim, however, there will not be enough of these people to go round, and this seems to be the current position in the fields of group work and community work.

With newer methods there is often some uncertainty about where the practitioners will fit into social work roles already established. If a new agency is created to provide the services, then there must be experimentation and some trial and error in working out appropriate organisational structures for the particular method. If the practitioners are to join an already established agency, again there is a period of some trial and error, as seen in the wide variety of ways in which local authority social service departments have introduced group workers into their hierarchies. For supervisors, whose roles relate so strongly to organisational lines of accountability, this period of experimentation and adjustment can be very trying.

As new methods are developed, many practitioners will wish to add skills in the new methods to their practice. This can provide problems for some supervisors who may know little of the new methods. Recent graduates who have experienced teaching from an integrated methods approach may have some knowledge and wish to develop more. Older workers may be eager to experiment. If the supervisor has had no teaching or experience in the new method, he cannot take on a teaching role; but he may still enable his workers to gain the experience by arranging consultation from an appropriate source.

In the area of student supervision, the shortage of qualified supervisors usually leads to a number of adjustments. For older methods such as casework a person supervising a student is usually required to hold a qualification which is at least the equivalent of the qualification for which the student is in training. For more recently developed methods, such a standard is a goal to be reached as soon as possible. In the meantime the few supervisors who are qualified are often over used, and both tutors and supervisors should be cautious about this. Naturally the supervisor will feel obliged to do as much as he possibly can to help get more people trained in his method, but there comes a point of diminishing returns if he tries to take on too many students. A valid compromise that is often used is to place the students with unqualified but experienced workers with a qualified supervisor taking responsibility for helping the workers to supervise the students. If there is no such person in the agency, then sometimes a tutor takes on this role or even spends a large part of his time in the field himself as a supervisor.

Supervision in Group Work

Supervision in group work is probably the closest to the casework model of any of the methods. Indeed Miller is particularly critical of the tendency of group work to rely too much on the casework model.[4] He suggests two major differences which should affect the style of supervision, the visibility of group work and the power of the group.

He points out that in most group work agencies there is considerable general knowledge of what goes on in groups. The members mix occasionally with members of other groups. They usually know most of the staff members including supervisors and director. When a meeting is over, if the group erupts happily or angrily into the halls, the supervisor will probably know. In some instances the supervisor may be a co-leader. In others, there may be many reasons for him to join the group for an occasional meeting.

Possibly because the work is so visible, there seems to be rather less structure at present for regular supervisory sessions in group work agencies. In some agencies where there are regular sessions, they have been found to be valuable, but they may be used differently from sessions in a casework setting. The need for reporting is not the same, but the need to review the work together thoughtfully remains. Similarly recording geared to point up the significant happenings in the group can provide an excellent base for thoughful discussion even though the supervisor was present during the action that was recorded.

In relation to the power of the group, Miller makes the point that the group is in a better position to defend itself against poor work than is the individual in a casework interview. He contrasts the group situation with that of a single client who may be overwhelmed by a caseworker whose education and experience may make the client feel and indeed be very vulnerable. The supervisor needs to be aware of what goes on in the interview not only to help the worker but to protect the client. It is certainly the responsibility of all supervisors to assure standards of service and thus protect the client. The group work supervisor cannot, however, depend entirely on the strength of the group to protect itself. The same power that allows a group to defend may at other times take over and render a worker ineffective so that the group may damage itself or some of its members. Of course an able worker will report such a situation to his supervisor, but a less able or inexperienced worker or student may not recognise what is happening. Like the casework supervisor, the group work supervisor needs to be aware of 'what goes on' not only to help the worker but to protect the clients. As we have already seen, his ways of assuring this awareness will differ slightly with the circumstances in which the work is done. Certainly a supervisor must guard against assigning either a worker or a student to a group whose problems are likely to be far beyond the coping capacities of the supervisee even with supervisory help.

Supervisors who are group workers, like supervisors in casework, need to use both individual and group methods when they are supervising several workers. In a group work agency it may be anticipated that both supervisor and workers will be comfortable with group supervision and able to make good use of it. There are times, however, when for any worker an individual session may be needed; and the supervisor should provide clear opportunity for such sessions. Usually students and new workers will need regular individual sessions as well as the group sessions. This, as will be shown in the chapters on student supervision and staff development, is geared to the different needs of each worker or student and which supplements the group teaching.

With the popularity of integrated teaching methods many casework supervisors may find themselves asked to give a student a group work experience in addition to casework. Similarly some staff supervisors may be supervising a worker who wishes to branch out and develop new skills by starting a group. Unless the supervisor happens to be a skilled group worker, he faces certain problems. Clearly the student supervisor should not agree to teach a student unless he has the requisite knowledge. Supervisors sometimes agreeably offer to let the student try to form a group 'just for the experience'. Too often the experience for both student and group members is a negative one. A supervisor without sound group work knowledge and experience cannot help a student effectively and may not recognise the dangers inherent in certain groupings. However, if there is someone within his agency who can provide the requisite knowledge and skill, it is quite proper for the supervisor to arrange for him to take responsibility for this part of the student's learning.

In the case of a worker who takes on group work, the situation is slightly different. The supervisor has responsibility for a general oversight of the worker's work. Providing the group work is relevant to the worker's assignment, it is certainly appropriate for the worker to develop his skills in this manner. The supervisor, if he is unable to help the worker in this area, should assist him in getting consultation from some other source. He should also make some effort to begin to learn something about group work himself. After all if he is responsible for assuring the standard of service to clients, he had better learn something about what those standards are in group work and what is necessary in the way of skills and resources to achieve them.

The Milieu for Supervision in Community Work

Supervision in community work is in as rapidly changing a state as community work itself. This youngest of the methods provides a stimulating but sometimes confused scene in which to practise supervision. Since the first Gulbenkian Report[5] provided a framework, the growth of community work in Great Britain has been impressive. That comprehensive report included, of course, much discussion of supervision and training. It was followed by a steady stream of conferences and reports which dealt most specifically with aspects of supervision in community work.[6] This is, perhaps, all the more surprising in that the generally activist philosophy of many community workers does not regard with enthusiasm such organisational concepts as bureaucracy, authority and accountability. Still community workers have seen that there is a need for supervision and have been rapidly developing a style suited to their own method.

This has not been easy and the task is far from completed. Community workers often work in comparative isolation and independence. Oddly enough the community worker is at the same time among the most visible of social workers and the most private. When he is conducting a public meeting or leading a demonstration, he is highly visible. When he is working with individuals or small groups to help them organise themselves for some community purpose, he may be very private indeed. Except occasionally for teaching purposes he is not usually required to keep a record of the details of his private work. In the discussion of group work the supervisor's dual responsibility to help the worker and to protect the client was mentioned. A community work supervisor in informal discussion with the author recently said: 'Well, I think I can tell by the results. If a worker has consciously or unconsciously manipulated a client for his own ends it will come out. The client just won't show up or will inexplicably not do something – inexplicably until we start examining the reasons together.' This is certainly one answer to the question of accountability and protection of the client. We will look at others in Part Two when we discuss accountability and reporting.

However, much of the work is highly visible. Very often the supervisor works alongside his workers in much the same way as described for group work. More often than not the supervisor will also be actively engaged in community work as well as having supervisory responsibilities. This may, on occasion, pose a special problem for him. As a worker he may be competing with other workers for resources. His tenant group may have a conflict of interest with another worker's recreation group. As a supervisor his responsibility is to facilitate his worker's practice, support his request for resources, and help him achieve the goals he has agreed with his group. Being fair and being seen to be fair may prove difficult.

Most staff supervisors in community work seem to rely more on group methods of supervision than on individual sessions. This fits in with the general philosophy and milieu of the work; and, as in group work, the supervisor may be expected to have some skill and confidence in working with a group. Perhaps more than supervisors in any other method, the community work supervisor must be prepared for worker challenges to his concept of his role. Community work attracts those who are primarily interested in working for social change. Such change rarely occurs without some questioning of authority and challenging of the status quo. The community work supervisor has now upon occasion to maintain the authority he questioned as a worker. He can and should be ready to change, be open to new ideas. However, he cannot abdicate all authority. He must come to terms with the implications of his responsibilities for administration and teaching as well as for enabling.

Community workers function frequently in less well defined situations than workers in other methods. In part this is due to the experimental nature of much of the practice. Boundaries and standards have not been agreed. The political implications are more intense than those encountered by other workers. The stress is often considerable, and the need for detached judgement may be an almost impossible demand in the heat of battle. The supervisor's supporting role is vital in such situations.

Here we come to another paradox. Just as the community worker is at once the most visible and most private of workers, so supervision may be the most intimate or most remote. On the one hand we have the stuation described – the supervisor working alongside his team. On the other, we find community workers outposted in remote settings with little contact with a supervisor located in 'head office'. The problem may be most acute in some national agencies when the head office is in London, but in a large local authority it can be almost as serious. It is also possible in the latter situation that the supervisor is not a community worker himself and so may have difficulty understanding some of the needs of the worker. In situations involving remote supervision, the supervision tends to be largely administrative. Perhaps the most the supervisor can do to provide support or teaching is to arrange for professional consultation at the local level, possibly similar to the Swiss developments.

Student Supervision in Community Work

Much of the writing on supervision in community work has centred on student supervision and strenuous efforts have been made to clarify the role. That some confusion remains probably results from two factors both related to the rapid development of this method. One factor is that the supply of fully qualified supervisors is so small. All the adaptations to such a' situation described previously are in use. Probably one of the chief demands on supervisors and tutors at present is to continue the attempts to spell out more precisely the areas for teaching and learning in the field. The framework for this was spelled out as early as the first Gulbenkian Report and has been repeated and refined in subsequent writings. The urgent need now is for these to be translated into teaching plans in the field relating to specific goals and students' individual capacities. Illustration of how this may be done will be found in Part Three.

The second factor leading to confusion has been the rapid rise in popularity of community work placements. Almost overnight it became *de rigueur* to send students for a community work placement. Students were often sent by tutors knowing little of the method themselves in the vague hope that they would 'learn something about community work'. The situation is gradually improving, but it is still all too possible that the community work supervisor will not be given appropriate information about the student or the guidance he should expect as to the goals of placement. Again this will be discussed in more detail in Part Three, but it is worth noting that the community work supervisor, far more than others, may have to sort out the different teaching requirements of the student who wishes to practise and the student who merely wishes to gain some knowledge of the method.

For those supervisors who may be supervising a student whose primary task is to learn a different method, the same steps will need to be taken as outlined at the end of the group work section.

RESIDENTIAL WORK

The Residential Milieu

Of all the methods discussed so far, it is in residential work that the most intimate proximity of supervisor and worker occurs. Beedell describes the complex of reactions and relationships that evolve from client and staff living together as the 'life-space situation'.[7] Ainsworth by use of diagrams shows the supervisor-student-client relationship in casework as a straight line, while the relationship of supervisor-student-resident is shown as circular.[8] All three are very much aware of one another's roles and activities within this life-space situation.

The residential worker is involved in the life of his clients far more intimately and for longer periods of time than are workers of any other method. He literally lives with them in an intimacy more prolonged than in other methods whether in fact he lives in the institution or not. The same is true for the supervisor. Both worker and supervisor must be aware of the interlocking social systems within the institution and the varying relationships within them. Inevitably the supervisor will know many personal things about the worker or student.

B

If the personal and professional are not to be inextricably mixed, it is important to define what are considered work areas and what actions or attributes of the worker may affect these areas. Delineation of tasks is essential and may be fairly straightforward. It is much more difficult to agree on what may affect these tasks. For instance a man may quarrel with his wife in privacy and yet carry on the next day with his work. If the quarrel, although happening in off-duty hours, is overheard by residents, may it affect their roles as house parents? The residential supervisor must make careful distinctions and must make sure his concerns are work related. Within the life-space situation the supervisor and worker must be particularly clear about accountability and authority for the comfort and security of the residents as well as themselves.

Because of the immediacy of living and working together, matters tend to get taken up as they arise rather than waiting for a formal supervisory session. The advantage is the supervisor's quick support and prompt decision. The disadvantage may be a loss of thoughtful discussion and planning unless the supervisor sets up sessions deliberately for this purpose. Even when they are regularly scheduled, supervisory sessions in the residential setting tend to be more open to interruption or cancellation than in, for example, a casework agency. Although it should be possible to hold to a timetable in this as in other activities, the climate of the work puts a priority on responding to many other living needs first. For many residential workers the informal chat over a cup of coffee after the children have been put to bed has provided a useful but limited substitute for more formal sessions. Where they have been arranged, regular sessions have proved a most useful device for focusing on professional rather than personal concerns.

In the larger residential establishments supervision may be carried out by someone in the usual mid-position, that is, the supervisor has workers accountable to him and is in turn accountable to the head. However, characteristically many residential institutions tend to be small; and in these it is often the head himself who supervises workers and often students as well. Much of his time must be taken up in administering the total institution, and supervision of workers is only part of his duties. His tasks will vary considerably from those of the casework supervisor. For example, the casework supervisor may have a task of assigning cases, but this does not usually include detailed spelling out of times and places for carrying out the tasks involved. The residential task includes timetabling with recognition of the worker's interests and capacities.

To date a very large percentage of residential staff is still untrained. This and the turnover of staff present special problems in supervision. Teaching may be a large part of the job, and yet this may be complicated by wide variation in motivation for learning on the part of staff. The close working together in the life-space situation is very much a plus in relation to the needs of new and untrained staff.

Student Supervision in Residential Placements

Residential supervisors suffer from some of the same problems as community work supervisors in the realm of student supervision. Again tutors are not always clear about what the goals of placement are, and there is a need to differentiate between placement of students who will become residential workers and those who want to learn something about residential work. Supervisors frequently complain that the information sent about students is insufficient for them to make valid judgements about how the student will fit into the residential community and what sort of tasks he may appropriately undertake. As we shall see in Part Three, the student supervisor in a residential placement must prepare the residents for the student's arrival to a far greater extent than the caseworker prepares individual clients. After all, as Ainsworth says, the residents are being asked to welcome a student to live in *their* home.[9]

CONTRASTS IN STAFF AND STUDENT SUPERVISION

In addition to differences with regard to method of practice, we must recognise that in all of the methods there are differences between staff and student supervision.

In Great Britain there has been more clarity about the role of the student supervisor than of the staff supervisor. In the early days in this country there was little staff supervision and what there was tended to concentrate on administrative responsibilities. Small agencies encouraged informal relationships. Supervisors with greater experience than their workers did offer some teaching and consultation but uneasily wondered if they had the 'right' to do so. Their duties were generally spelled out in administrative terms; yet there was a general expectation that they would 'help' their workers.

In those same early days much writing and discussion was focused on student supervision. The Home Office sponsored courses throughout the country on student supervision. Tutors and supervisors met together to decide on tasks and role. Although various supervisors saw their roles somewhat differently, on the whole the student supervisor did not receive the sort of imprecise message that was given to the staff supervisor.

In the past decade more attention has been paid to staff supervision, and courses and workshops have been offered. Student supervisors, too, have continued to clarify their role and function. While there is much greater understanding of all supervision today than in the past, it is probably true to say that there is still more general agreement about expectations of student supervision than of staff supervision.

One of the chief differences in function is that the student supervisor has a dual accountability to both agency and course. The student supervisor, as a member of staff, is accountable to his own agency. If he assigns work to the student, he is responsible for seeing that the standards of the agency are maintained, that the clients are well served. At the same time he is accountable to the course from which the student is placed. He is responsible for providing teaching for the student, for following an agreed plan of providing learning opportunities. In this context of accountability, his role is therefore more complex than that of the staff supervisor.

Both staff and student supervisors must use skills in administration and teaching. If there is a difference here, it may be in the priority given to one or the other. Probably the first priority in staff supervision is the administrative or management tasks, with staff development an important and essential adjunct. In student supervision, the teaching tasks have first priority but cannot be accomplished without fulfilling administrative and management aspects.

CONCLUSIONS

The basic concepts of supervision hold for all methods. The worker or student is accountable to the supervisor. The supervisor is responsible for helping worker or student to practise to the best of his ability and will use skills in administration, teaching, enabling and communication plus knowledge of social work to do so.

However, it is important to be clear about those aspects of supervision that are different for different methods. Too often assumptions have been made upon the basis of the casework model when this has been quite inappropriate to another method of practice. We have seen that differences in supervisory style relate usefully to the differences in milieu in which the various methods are practised. If the supervisor is task focused, aware of his workers as individuals, and aware of his milieu, he will use the basic tenets of supervision flexibly and appropriately in all methods.

REFERENCES

1 Charlotte Towle, 'The Place of Help in Supervision', *The Social Service Review*, vol. 38, no. 4 (1963), or in *Education for Social Work*, edited by Eileen Younghusband, George Allen & Unwin (1968).
2 Lucille Austin, 'An Evaluation of Supervision', *Social Casework*, vol. 37, no. 8 (1956), and *Case Conference*, vol. 3, no. 8 (1957).

3   *Sozialarbeit Travail Social,* op. cit.
4   Irving Miller, 'Distinctive Characteristics of Supervision in Group Work',
    Social Work (U.S.), vol. 5, no. 1 (1960).
5   Gulbenkian Group, Eileen Younghusband, Chairman, *Community Work and
    Social Change,* Longman (1968).
6   See Gulbenkian Group (1968), op. cit.; *Supervision of Community Work
    Students,* report of a seminar sponsored by the Standing Councils of Social
    Service (1969); *Fieldwork Supervision for Community Work Students,* report
    of a consultation sponsored by National Council of Social Service (1970);
    Supervision in Community Work Placements, report of a day study consultation
    sponsored by the Joint University Council for Social and Public Administration
    (1972); Gulbenkian Group, Lord Boyle, Chairman, *Current Issues in Community
    Work,* Routledge & Kegan Paul (1973); CCETSW Community Work Study
    Group, *The Teaching of Community Work* (1975); and Catherine Briscoe and
    David Thomas, *Community Work: Learning and Supervision,* George Allen &
    Unwin (1977).
7   Christopher Beedell, *Residential Life with Children,* Routledge & Kegan Paul
    (1970).
8   Frank Ainsworth and N. Bridgeford, 'Student Supervision in Residential Work',
    The British Journal of Social Work, vol. 1, no. 4 (1971).
9   ibid.

FURTHER READING

J. Cheetham and M. Hill, 'Community Work: Social Realities and Ethical
    Dilemmas', *The Journal of British Social Work,* vol. 3, no. 3 (1973).
Barbara Holmes, Richard Bryant and Donald Houston, 'Student Unit in Community
    Work: An Experimental Approach', *Social Work Today,* vol. 4, no. 14 (1973).
G. Knopka, *Social Groupwork,* Prentice Hall (1972).
Herbert Laming and Sheila Stanton, 'The Development of Groupwork in a Social
    Service Department', *Social Work Today,* vol. 8, no. 4 (1977).
Chris Payne, 'Caring for the Care-Givers', *Social Work Today,* vol. 8, no. 15
    (1977).
Gerald Popplestone, 'The Ideology of Professional Community Workers', *The
    British Journal of Social Work,* vol. 1, no. 1 (1971).
Angela Rigby, 'Residential Placements', *Social Work Today,* vol. 3, no. 11 (1972).
Harry Specht and Anne Vickery, *Integrating Social Work Methods,* George Allen
    & Unwin (1977).
Sheila Sturton, 'Developing Groupwork in a Casework Agency', *The British Journal
    of Social Work,* vol. 2, no. 2 (1972).
Joan M. Tash, *Supervision in Youth Work,* The National Council of Social Service
    (1967).
David M. Thomas and R. William Warburton, 'Community Workers in a Social
    Services Department', *Social Work Today,* vol. 9, no. 3 (1977).
Ellis Thorpe, 'Community Work Training: A Not to be Taken for Granted World',
    Social Work Today, vol. 2, no. 5 (1971).
Anne Vickery, 'A Systems Approach to Social Work Intervention: Its Uses for
    Work with Individuals and Families', *The Journal of British Social Work,* vol.
    4, no. 4 (1974).

Liz Ward, 'Communications Plus: The Key to Residential Work', *Social Work Today*, vol. 6, no. 2 (1975); 'Clarifying the Residential Social Work Task', *Social Work Today*, vol. 9, no. 9 (1977); 'Supervising Students in a Residential Setting', *Social Work Today*, vol. 9, no. 10 (1977).

Dorothy Stock Whitaker, 'Some Conditions for Effective Work with Groups', *The British Journal of Social Work*, vol. 5, no. 4 (1975).

PART TWO:
STAFF SUPERVISION

INTRODUCTION

In Part Two the focus will be on the role and tasks related to staff supervision. A discussion of student supervision will follow in Part Three. Staff supervision requires a heavy investment in both administrative and teaching functions. The supervisor works with individuals and groups, and his working relationships are formed within a hierarchical structure. It is necessary for purposes of discussion to divide the multi-faceted roles and functions, although in actual practice they are inextricably intertwined. Indeed, so intertwined are they, that one must arbitrarily select the division and order of presentation. The initial focus in Chapter 3 will be on the roles and duties of a staff supervisor or team leader within the agency structure. Chapters 4 and 5 will deal with his tasks relating to individual workers, first the administrative tasks and then the teaching tasks. Finally, Chapter 6 is devoted to his work with his team in both management and staff development areas. The order of presentation relates neither to the importance of the skills involved nor the difficulties of the tasks. All are essential for effective supervision.

Chapter 3

INTRODUCTION TO STAFF SUPERVISION

Supervision of staff may mean supervising a team of several workers or only one or two workers, depending on the size of the agency and the kind of assignment that has been made. Supervision of workers, as we have seen, characteristically involves enabling those workers *who are accountable to the supervisor* to function effectively. This chapter will describe some of the duties and expectations generally ascribed to those who supervise staff. In subsequent chapters the tasks involved (the 'how' of the duties) will be discussed.

WHO IS THE TEAM LEADER OR STAFF SUPERVISOR?

Confusion of Terms
The terms used to designate those with staff supervisory responsibilities in the social services seem to be used interchangeably to describe varying levels of authority and responsiblity. This is particularly notice-able in the local authority social services departments since the Seebohm reorganisation. 'Team leader', for instance, is often used to describe either the leader of an area team (which may include several smaller teams) or the leader of a team of basic grade social workers within the area team. 'Senior' for many years was used to designate the leader of a team of basic grade social workers, and in some places it still is. On the other hand it is now frequently the term for career grade specialist practitioners with no supervisory responsibilities. There seems little agreement on what constitutes a team. All the workers in an area office may be referred to as the area team, but this group may be broken down into smaller teams. These may be formed on a geographical base such as a section of a community or a ward of a hospital, or the division may be by work classification such as an intake team or a team of health workers. Sometimes the team seems to consist simply of those persons assigned to a given 'leader'.

Definition of Terms
This book is addressed primarily to those supervisors who are responsible

for social workers or students functioning as practitioners (of whatever method) at the operational level.

The term 'team leader' will be used throughout to refer to the leader of a team of such workers. Normally a team consists of some five to eight persons, the majority of whom may be social workers, although some teams may include social work assistants, occupational therapists, trainee social workers, and so forth.

The term 'staff supervisor' will refer to the those persons who may have supervisory responsibility for one or two members of staff. Normally they will have other duties as well, but at least part of their time will be devoted to supervision of one or two staff members directly accountable to them.

The generic term 'supervisor' will be used for anyone who supervises either staff or students and will be used interchangeably with team leader, staff supervisor or student supervisor. The focus will be on supervisory practice related to those persons, be they staff or students, who are practising at the operational level. However, much of what is written will also apply to leaders of larger units such as area directors and heads of residential establishments. A rough rule of thumb is that the larger the number of workers for whom a supervisor is responsible, the greater the focus of his supervisory practice is on management content.

EXPECTATIONS ARISING FROM JOB DESCRIPTIONS

Job Descriptions

A composite description of duties (based on a number of such descriptions reviewed by the author) would include the following:

(1) Give leadership to a team of workers.
(2) Ensure that statutory requirements are met and records and statistics maintained.
(3) Maintain professional standards.
(4) Allocate work.
(5) Perform standby duty as required.
(6) Carry a small caseload.
(7) Undertake special duties as required.

Details vary. Some local authorities spell these out in a long list of specific responsibilities; others simply list the general duties. Not all require 'a small caseload', but a great many do list this. The first four relate specifically to supervisory practice; and the fifth probably does, if the assumption is that the team leader would be undertaking standby duty in his supervisory capacity. Expectations arising from these five listed duties fall into three categories of knowledge, activities and accountability, making heavy demands on the team leader's time and energy.

Expectation of Knowledge

The supervisor is expected to have knowledge of what needs to be done. To know this he must understand the policies and functions of his agency, what it has been set up to do, and what statutory requirements govern the work. Within this general framework what, specifically, are his team's responsibilities? What are the boundaries of the team's work – either geographically or by types of cases? Is there a responsibility for searching out areas of need? Is there a responsibility for referring applicants elsewhere if their requests do not come within agency function? What types of services should or may be offered? The team leader is expected to have the answers to these questions.

He must have knowledge, too, of how the work is done. The team leader must not only know what needs to be done, he must assure himself that it is done and done to standard. This implies that he will know what standards are expected in his agency. Unless he has a very small team and they carry miniscule caseloads, he cannot be expected to know the details of every case. Yet he is expected to have knowledge of what each worker is doing, what progress has been made, what has been achieved or completed. In addition he is expected to know how the work is being done – by what methods, using what resources, and of what quality. To achieve even a minimum knowledge in these areas he must spend considerable time reviewing work. He must set up ways in which workers can report to him orally or in writing. Without this knowledge he would have difficulty allocating work fairly, and it would be impossible to give assurance regarding either professional standards or statutory requirements.

Again he must have knowledge of resources, which may include a vast variety of means for getting work done. Manpower is a resource. The team leader must have knowledge of the variations of skill and capacity of the individual team members, if he is to deploy this resource successfully. Time is a most precious resource, and the team leader who can help his team organise time effectively makes available to them a vital resource. Financial resources come in many forms within and without the agency. The supervisor is expected to have knowledge of a wide variety of resources and the ways in which they may be used.

Expectations Regarding Team Leader's Activities

Some activities have been mentioned already in relation to the knowledge the team leader needs. In addition, the duties set forth by most agencies imply activities in managerial, teaching and supporting functions. The team leader is expected to organise the work of the team (and help his workers organise their work) so that it may be most effectively accomplished. He is expected to set standards. When it is necessary, he is expected to become a teacher to enable a worker to reach professional standards. He is expected to be available for consultation, to answer questions and to make decisions. Implicit in all of this is the expectation of clear communication.

Expectation of Accountability
The expectation of accountability runs through all of the duties listed. The team leader is expected to hold his workers accountable for doing assigned work according to statutory requirements and agency standards. He, too, is accountable to his superiors within the agency for the discharge of the duties assigned to him, and he must show that he has done so. None of the supervisory duties discussed so far, or the expectations arising from them, involve the team leader in responsibility for direct work with clients. His accountability, it would seem, must chiefly be concerned with fulfilling those duties that make it possible for the team to work effectively with clients.

CONFLICT OF DEMANDS

Other duties may be required of the team leader or staff supervisor besides those most directly related to the supervisory role. One of the most frequently assigned of such duties is that of carrying a small caseload, yet it is this assignment that is most likely to make demands upon him that will severely conflict with his supervisory responsibilities. It is important here to differentiate between the team leader and staff supervisor. The duties required of a team leader and the expectations arising from them constitute a full-time job in relation to a team of any size at all. The staff supervisor, who is supervising but one or two workers is almost by definition a part-time supervisor. He will have more time to devote to a variety of duties and to sorting out any conflicts of interest which may arise. It is necessary, therefore, to discuss the addition of a caseload to either of these two roles separately.

Should the Team Leader Carry a Small Caseload?
The reason most often given for such an assignment is that it keeps the team leader in touch with practice. Workers who are about to become supervisors are often most reluctant to give up direct work with clients. They may feel a certain loyalty to some clients already in their caseload. In addition they fear loss of satisfaction and of hard-won skills. They do not realise that as supervisors they will still be in touch with

practice, still using their skills, but in a different way. A 'small' caseload does little to keep one in touch with the multi-faceted aspects of practice. At best the team leader can work with only a very few cases at a time. On the other hand, as he consults with the various members of the team about the practice problems they will inevitably bring, he finds himself in touch with not only a wide range of problems but a wide variety of ways of coping. His knowledge of the possibilities of practice will be greatly enriched. Skills he developed as a caseworker will still be used. The art of building relationships need not be confined to client relationships. Relationships with colleagues – whether they be team members, representatives of other disciplines, or members of a community committee – require skill and perception and self-control as much as the client-centred relationship. Understanding of human behaviour, assessment of intricate situations, seeing the relationship of parts to the whole and cause and effect – all demand the same skills that were developed in practice but must be used differently. The use of these skills need not and must not lead to 'caseworking the caseworker'. As the team leader begins to understand the objectives of his work as team leader, he will use his skills to attain these appropriate objectives and not for therapeutic purposes.

If the team leader does not need a small caseload to keep in touch with practice, it is hard to justify the use of his time in this manner. Of all his possible assignments, a caseload appears to present the greatest conflict in regard to demands. Presumably, as leader of a team, he must rate the needs of his team above all others when establishing priorities of time and commitment. Yet for a professional social worker, the needs of his clients should come first. As far as it is possible to schedule home visits and supervisory sessions, it may be argued that a reasonable amount of time might be allotted to each. However, crises do arise all too frequently, and it is not inconceivable that while the team leader is off dealing with his client's crisis, three workers are handicapped in dealing with their clients' crisis because of his unavailability. The client's needs come first – but which client, the team leader's or those of his workers? It must be obvious that when one takes on the role of team leader, the first responsibility is to one's team.

Other assignments may be more appropriate than carrying a small caseload. Most team leaders are expected to take on some peripheral assignments; and if these can be contained in planned periods of time at relatively fixed intervals, there is less conflict of demand upon the team leader. Such assignments as court liaison officer, housing officer, or licensing child minders can usually be fitted into the overall organisation of his time. Representing the agency on certain community committees is another way of giving additional service. Teaching in in-service training programmes or consultation in areas of expertise to groups outside the department are further appropriate activities. Whatever the assignment, it should be worked out in relation to the demands of the team leader's primary responsibility to his team.

Differing Demands on Staff Supervisors

The staff supervisor is in a rather different situation from the team leader in that he is in essence a part-time supervisor. Basically he carries on his practice as a social worker, but in addition he supervises one or two other workers. This kind of assignment is found in all methods of social work, but it is less frequently used in casework because the sheer number of workers tends to make organisation of work by teams more feasible.

It is necessary for the staff supervisor carefully to assess the amount of time needed to fulfil his dual responsibilities and to arrange his timetable accordingly. In view of the responsibility of any supervisor to be be available for consultation and decisions, frequent opportunities for contact with workers are essential in addition to regular supervisory sessions.

Because the staff supervisor may focus for much of the time on his own practice, he will need consciously to change roles when consulting with one of his workers. He must not ask himself, 'What would I do?', but rather, 'What can the worker do?'. At times, too, he may find himself as a worker competing with workers accountable to him for scarce resources, for example, a bed for an elderly client or a place at a holiday camp for a child. He must be fair and be seen to be fair. He may need to seek a group decision or to consult a third party.

IMPLICATIONS OF MID-POSITION

Accountability

We saw in Chapter 1 that a team leader or supervisor is usually in a mid-position. He has some people accountable to him, and he is accountable to someone else. Unfortunately accountability to whom and for what is not always clear. Workers are sometimes unclear whether they are immediately accountable to their supervisor or to the area director. Team leaders are unsure of their authority regarding certain areas of work. Rowbottom and his colleagues noted several instances of such confusion in their studies of social services departments.[1] The author has noticed similar confusion in response to questionnaires used over a period of years asking persons planning to come on courses in supervision to whom they are accountable and who is accountable to them. It has, however, been noticeable that in recent years there have been fewer confused answers. As reorganisation has followed reorganisation, there have been increasing attempts to spell out organisational roles and accountability; and less is taken for granted.

Certainly a first requisite for anyone undertaking supervisory duties is to clarify to whom he is accountable and for what and who is accountable to him and for what. While one would assume that management decisions would already have set out clear lines of accountability, in practice this is not always so; and the new supervisor may find that persons at different levels in the hierarchy are making quite contradictory assumptions about his responsibilities or authority. Normally a team leader will be directly accountable to an area officer or, in the case of a small agency, to the director; but in other situations there may be a confusing variety of structures. A community work supervisor outposted in a special area may find himself directly accountable to an area officer or an assistant director of community work at head office. A supervisor of medical social workers may be directly accountable to the principal medical social worker or to an area director or to both for different aspects of the work. The person supervising basic grade workers in a residential establishment may well be the head of the establishment who may be accountable to a board or to the assistant director of residential work or to an area officer, depending on the structure of the local authority for whom he works. All this is further complicated if the team leader has taken on special assignments which may mean he is accountable to someone else for that area of work. Whatever the situation may be, the important thing is that all concerned understand the lines of accountability. If the supervisor is to be accountable to more than one person, then it is well to remember the administrative concept of the 'cross-over point' – that the final accountability must rest with a person in a position of authority over both persons to whom the supervisor is accountable.

In the questionnaires mentioned previously, several supervisors answered that they felt accountable not only to someone in a post above them but to their workers as well. Although this is rarely pictured in flow charts of accountability or authority, the concept is valid. Team members have a right to expect certain things from their team leaders, including a basic assumption that the team leader will do his job as well as he expects his workers to do theirs. A part of that job is sorting out with the worker what each may expect of the other – in other words, 'accountability and for what'.

The Linking Role

The mid-position between the operational worker and those concerned with management is both a vital and a difficult role. Workers and management have been known to speak of each other as 'we' and 'they', and it may sometimes appear to the supervisor that whichever group is speaking he is always 'they'. Yet actually the opposite should be true. If he is to carry out his linking role, he must thoroughly understand the concerns and needs of both. He is part of management and as such will share in management goals. He must be aware of policies to implement these goals and aware of the problems management faces in bringing workers and resources together in an effective design to provide the services for which the agency is responsible. Equally he is concerned with practice. Here he needs to be aware of the possibilities of service, to know what goes into making a good diagnosis or assessment, to appreciate what skills and resources are needed for effective practice.

Communications or the Gate-Keeping Role

If it is part of the supervisor's task to understand policies and how they relate to overall goals, it is also his task to communicate this understanding to workers and to communicate how the policies are working to management. In communicating his understanding of policies, he is drawing on knowledge based in management responsibilities. In communicating how policies are working out, he is drawing on his knowledge of practice.

If it is part of his task to be concerned about resources, it follows that his communication will again be concerned with both aspects. On the basis of his knowledge of practice, his understanding of what the team members are attempting, he will communicate what resources are needed, be it ball-point pens, nursing-home beds, time or training courses. He will also be reporting unmet needs, and from his knowledge of management exploring ways of meeting the needs. Since this is a far from perfect world, he will spend much of his time communicating to workers the limits of resources available and again using his practice knowledge to help them work as effectively as possible within these limits.

If management is to function effectively, it must have accurate knowledge of what work is being done and to what standard. It must have assessments of the effectiveness of the work. It must be aware both of clients' needs and of workers' needs. Management looks to the team leader's assessments and reports as a major source of precise information for planning and implementation of service delivery.

If workers are to function effectively, they must be provided with the resources of knowledge, time, organisational backing and the infinite variety of tools for the job that may be required. It is the team leader's responsibility to bring these needs to the attention of management.

Effective flow of communication is essential in a complex organisation such as most social work agencies now are. The person in a mid-position is the key to how effective the flow may be. Persons at both ends of the hierarchy can start the flow, but whether the information so embarked reaches the other end and in what form will depend upon the way it is handled en route. The role of the discriminating gate-keeper is essential. It is obvious that if too little information gets through, there can be difficulty. It may seem less obvious that there can be too much information, yet too much information can block efficient functioning. In a large organisation where various persons have different functions to perform, each will need the information essential to his particular functioning, and he will certainly need to understand the functioning of others as it relates to his own. He cannot function in isolation, yet he must have a chance to concentrate upon his own tasks. If the flow of information is blocked by a narrow or closed gate no one can function effectively. If on the other hand the team leader pushes all information upward or downward without discrimination, the flood may well overwhelm its recipients. His is a screening responsibility, and it leaves him with a very considerable influence for good or ill.

Nowhere is the gate-keeping role more important than in the decision-making process. Organisations usually delegate authority to make decisions along a hierarchical line with different posts carrying with them the authority for making certain types of decisions. This can rarely be spelled out so perfectly that there is clear-cut understanding in all instances, and this is particularly so where professional judgements may be involved. The team leader or supervisor will have authority to make certain but not all decisions. Perhaps the greatest test of his judgement and decision-making capacities comes in those circumstances when he must make decisions about what to pass on to higher authority and what to delegate to others. Guidelines to the decision-making process will be discussed in the next chapter. It is mentioned here because of its relevance to the supervisor's mid-position. Because of this mid-position, he is frequently required to make judgements as to where decisions should be made.

PARTICIPATION IN MANAGEMENT

The team leader's participation in management will vary with the size and structure of the agency in which he works. Where area offices are regarded as mini-departments, the participation may sometimes be quite considerable. In one such agency known to the author, the team leaders have only one step between themselves and overall management. The top management team is formed of area directors meeting with the director, and overall decisions are taken at this level. Within each area office, the area director forms his own management team of team leaders. These area management teams meet weekly, and all area policy and decisions are made at this level. The team leaders meeting with their area director can raise any matters with him they wish to have taken up at the top management meetings. These team leaders are, then, intimately involved in management matters; and since they also hold regular meetings with their own teams, the result is that workers at the operational level have a fairly short line to top management.

In other circumstances a team leader may find himself in a remote area office where the area director makes little effort to involve his team leaders in management matters, or where the area director may have little management responsibility himself, having to refer most matters through a complicated hierarchy at head office.

Most often the team leader finds himself in a position somewhere between these two extremes. It is difficult to say what might be considered ideal. The team leader needs a considerable amount of time to devote to his team members both as individuals and as a group. If he is asked to devote too much of his time to management concerns, this side of his work could suffer, and he may make less informed contributions to management decisions because he lacks sufficient direct contact with staff in practice. On the other hand the supervisor or team leader able to influence management decisions and to participate in planning can far more effectively help his team than one who is cut off from such aspects. It is, as we have seen, a vital part of his responsibilities to form a link between management and operational level, and to do this he must have access to both. Many team leaders have a formal structure of participation through management meetings. Most staff supervisors and some team leaders who do not have this sort of structure available do at least have the opportunity to carry out this part of their responsibilities in regularly scheduled individual sessions with someone to whom they are accountable. The old-fashioned system of simply catching one's superior when possible and usually only for emergency decisions is simply not good enough for a modern social work organisation.

This brings us to the subject of the support which a team leader or supervisor may expect from the person to whom he is accountable. A new supervisor should be given considerable support as he learns the demands of his new assignment. His questions should be answered, guidance and advice offered. Very often he may find himself in the position of his student days, saying 'I don't know, but I'll find out', only now he will be saying it to workers instead of clients. Inevitably he will take more time with his area officer than a more experienced supervisor. It is the same as with a new worker or beginning student. Eventually the supervisor will be expected to have learned sufficient to act with increasing independence. He may or may not find that he has regular sessions with his superior as often as his workers have with him. Hopefully he and his area director will work out what is necessary and useful together, just as the supervisor will do with his workers. As in all such situations, what may be agreed will vary with the duties and capacities of the individuals concerned. How the supervisor works with the individuals in his team will be discussed in the following chapters.

CONCLUSIONS

The team leader or supervisor of basic grade workers holds a vital role. The position is difficult if he has to carry assignments that are not well defined or pose conflicting demands. The team leader must give his supervisorial duties priority if he is to accomplish his task of welding managerial support to operational goals. In his mid-position judgement and discretion in his gate-keeping role are essential. His concern and participation in management will enhance his capacity to help his team practise effectively. His knowledge of what is effective in practice, based on close working relations with his team, will enhance his contribution to management.

REFERENCE

1 Rowbottom, Hey and Billis, *Social Service Departments*, Heinemann (1974), ch. 5.

FURTHER READING

E. T. Ashton, 'The Application of Management Theory in the Social Services', *Social Work* (British), vol. 24, no. 2 (1967).

Jonathan G. Bailey, 'A Systematic Approach to Training Area Officers', *Social Work Today*, vol. 1, no. 9 (1970).

Arthur K. Berliner, 'Some Pitfalls in Administrative Behaviour', *Social Casework*, vol. 52, no. 11 (1971).

Anne Chrichton, 'Training for Management in the Social Services', *Social Work* (British), vol. 24, no. 2 (1967).

Bryan Glastonbury, 'The Social Worker: "Cannon Fodder in the Age of Administration"?', *Social Work Today*, vol. 6, no. 10 (1975).

E. Goldberg, R. William Warburton, Brendon McGuinness and John H. Rowlands, 'Towards Accountability in Social Work: One Year's Intake in an Area Office', *The Brtish Journal of Social Work*, vol. 7, no. 3 (1977).

W. Hampton, 'Working with Administration', *Case Conference*, vol. 12, no. 10 (1966).

Brian Harrison, 'Staff Supervision', *FSU Quarterly*, no. 12 (Winter 1977).

Kevin Heal, 'Conflict and the Social Service Department', *Social Work Today*, vol. 1, no. 11 (1971).

Ralph L. James, 'Management by Objectives', *Social Work Today*, vol. 6, no. 21 (1976).

Tony Jones, 'The Senior Social Worker Within the Area Structure', *Social Work Today*, vol. 8, no. 32 (1977).

Mark Monger, *Casework in Probation*, Butterworth (1964), last three chapters.

E. C. Morris, Editor, *Social Work Service*, no. 6 (June 1975). (The whole issue is devoted to the delivery of the social services.)

Rolf Olsen, Editor, *Management in the Social Services – The Team Leader's Task* (Occasional Papers no. 1), University of North Wales (1975).

R. A. Packer, 'Social Administration and Scarcity: The Problem of Rationing', *Social Work* (British), vol. 24, no. 2 (1967).

Margaret Pickering, 'Realities of Work in an Area Team', *Social Work Today*, vol. 6, no. 13 (1975).

Maurice Phillips and Elizabeth Burchill, 'Structuring an Area Office to Meet Client Need', *Social Work Today*, vol. 1, no. 10 (1971).

Ruth Popplestone, 'Paired Supervision', *FSU Quarterly*, No. 12 (Winter 1977).

Kay Richards, 'The New Social Service Departments; Practical Problems in Planning Objectives and Priorities', *Social Work Today*, vol. 2, no. 1 (1972).

I. F. Shaw, 'Agency Decentralisation: Planning and Assessment', *The British Journal of Social Work*, vol. 3, no. 2 (1973).

Frances Sherz, 'A Concept of Supervision Based on a Definition of Job Responsibility', *Social Casework*, vol. 39, no. 8 (1958).

Duncan Smith, 'Communication and Change in the Social Services', *Social Work* (British), vol. 24, no. 2 (1967).

G. Smith and R. Harris, 'Ideologies of Need and the Organisation of Social Work Departments', *TheJournal of British Social Work*, vol. 2, no. 1 (1972).

Shirley Weber and Donald Polm, 'Participatory Management in Public Welfare', *Social Casework*, vol. 55, no. 5 (1974).

Chapter 4

MANAGEMENT TASKS RELATED TO INDIVIDUAL WORKERS

The supervisor's responsibility to participate in management and his responsibility to the levels above him have been outlined in the previous chapter. He has equal responsibility to his workers. If they are accountable to him for the work that they do, he is responsible to them for letting them know what work is to be done. Many of his activities will be related to enabling the workers to get the work done. He will be giving guidelines as to standards and providing a channel by which the work may be perceived to be done and assessed. We will look in this chapter at tasks designed to enable workers to make use of supervision, to facilitate good decision taking, to provide a structure for knowing about the work, and to participate in evaluation as part of management. All of these relate specifically to individual workers. Allocation of work, which is certainly individual in one sense, will be discussed in relation to group supervision since it is a matter which also concerns the total team, as does the provision of resources.

ENABLING THE WORKER TO USE SUPERVISION

Workers of all degrees of experience and training have a right to have appropriate supervision available to them in the often complex and difficult area of administration and management of their work. This may appear obvious, yet the realisation of this aim requires some thought and effort by both participants in the worker/supervisor relationship. Basically, by spelling out organisational roles and expectations, management will have given the supervisor and worker a framework for working together and understanding what they may expect of each other. If the supervisor is to offer the opportunity of a really effective worker/supervisor relationship, he must keep three things in mind. First, his supervision must be sufficiently flexible to meet the varying requirements of each individual worker. Second, the worker must have some assurance of regular contact with his supervisor. Finally, the authority inherent in the relationship needs to be mutually recognised and used as a constructive element in working together.

Flexible Supervision from a Consistent Base

The supervisor's task here is to offer an opportunity for each worker to decide with him how much and what type of supervision is necessary and useful. It may seem attractive to suggest that every worker in a team be treated alike – each worker to have the same amount of time regularly available for supervisory sessions, everyone to go to the supervisor for certain authorisations and the like. Given the variety of training and abilities represented in most teams, this is neither fair to the individual worker nor an effective use of the supervisor's time.

The young and inexperienced worker will usually need more supervisory attention than the older, experienced worker, but far more differentiation is needed than is provided by these two broad categories. One worker may require help from his supervisor mainly with administrative details, while another may be most knowledgeable in this area but unsure in his direct work with clients. One may wish to use his supervisor as a sounding-board; another may require considerable direct teaching.

In working out the amount and kind of supervision needed, not only the worker's requirements but the supervisor's, too, should be considered. As we have seen, the supervisor needs to know about the work and how it is being carried out. He is dependent on this knowledge to carry out many of his various responsibilities. He will be influenced by his assessment of the worker's capabilities as to how much and how frequently he may need to review the work. With a worker new to him, he will probably feel the need for more direct knowledge of his current work than with one with whom he has worked for some time.

As we look at the various factors that may influence the amount and kind of supervision needed, it becomes evident that not only does it vary from worker to worker, but the same worker may present changing requirements over a period of time. A flexible supervisor will work out with each of his workers an agreed method of working together, but leave it open for review as the situation changes. The most recognisable variable in this process is the frequency of supervisory sessions.

Regular Supervisory Sessions

If the worker is to have assurance of regular contact with his supervisor, it is necessary to set a timetable for supervisory sessions. The frequency and content of the sessions may be varied according to what may be deemed most effective individually, but some time should be set aside on a regular planned basis for each worker. In the past some supervisors did not recognise the need for regular sessions.

In an effort to provide flexibility according to the workers' needs, they offered an 'open door' policy so that workers might make use of supervision 'as needed'.

Such a policy rarely achieves its objectives. It overlooks the point that supervision sessions are a planned two-way task. The team leader as well as the worker may have things he needs to discuss. In addition, realistically, an 'open door' cannot be open all the time. When one worker is inside, others cannot be. It leaves the team leader open to interruption and unable to undertake any sustained commitment to other work. The result is that in reality there will be long periods when the door cannot be open.

For both worker and supervisor a regularly scheduled time holds many benefits. It is a time they can count on for dealing with those things about which they will need to consult. The sessions provide a framework for planning; each can decide – and, indeed, they can decide together – what needs to be done before the next session. Inevitably crises will occasionally arise that prevent them from keeping to the allotted time; but when this happens, a new time should usually be set rather than just cancelling the session.

The most usual time interval between sessions is one week, but this need not necessarily be so for all workers. The one-week interval follows the normal practice of student supervision, and it has been found to be a good interval of time for any worker who still has a fair amount of learning to do. Those working more independently may still need a weekly interval to clear various administrative matters, but for others two-weekly intervals or even, in a few instances, a monthly interval, may be sufficient. How often the supervisor and worker should meet will be determined by what needs to be done. Whatever the pattern set, it should be reviewed from time to time. If the sessions are continuing productively, the timing is correct. If there is not enough to talk about during the sessions, perhaps a longer interval or planned shorter sessions may be appropriate. If, on the other hand, there never seems to be enough time to complete discussions and the worker must frequently come between sessions, then perhaps more frequent sessions are needed. Obviously in such cases the supervisor will need to look first at how well both he and the worker are using the sessions. There may be little to talk about because the worker is unwilling to bring things for discussion. The crowded sessions may be so because they allow themselves to wander from the point.

The content of the sessions will vary. Sometimes they may focus largely on administrative matters; sometimes teaching or support may be paramount. In the following subsections on decision making, reporting and evaluation we will see many examples of how the supervisory sessions may be used for these processes. Whatever the focus of the sessions, their regularity and continuity provide opportunity for mutual learning and effective working. As worker and supervisor experience the value of working together in this way, constructive use of supervision may become an attained goal.

The Use and Abuse of Authority

Authority is implicit and explicit in the role of the supervisor and the attitudes of both the worker and supervisor to authority will affect the use of supervision.

The supervisor's authority rests in his position. In any hierarchical organisation authority is assigned to various posts, but authority is never absolute. Within the administrative structure there will be provision for questioning decisions or demands. Ultimately the use of authority rests upon recognition by the worker and supervisor that authority is being properly used. The assmption is that by taking employment in an organisation the various members implicitly agree to the normal and reasonable use of authority within the administrative structure. The supervisor, then, can be expected to exercise his authority with regard to the work situation with some degree of confidence. It is his responsibility to use his authority in such a way as to ensure effective working. He may, for example, set up duty rosters to ensure adequate coverage or require certain types of reporting so that it can be known what work has been accomplished.

In addition to the authority inherent in the position, there may also be authority based on knowledge as well as charismatic or personal authority. These will obviously vary, and the authority of each supervisor will be based on a unique blend of his status, knowledge and personality. The supervisor need not and cannot know more about everything than his workers. In some areas he will have more knowledge. Such knowledge adds an increased authority to his opinion or decision.

A supervisor's use of authority for the most part remains un-obtrusive. It is there in the background, and the implicit contracts are honoured. It is when there is some challenge to the authority or authority is misused that it becomes apparent. Authority may be misused if it is not used reasonably or if it is used for personal satisfaction rather than for furtherance of work. What may be 'reasonable' is, of course, a matter of personal judgement and opinion, but the supervisor needs to be sensitive to what may be commonly accepted custom within his agency.

Supervisors may meet challenges to their authority in a variety of ways. Discussion with the worker is an obvious step. Is this a difference of opinion that may be resolved? Humour, persuasion or consultation with others may be involved. In some cases it may be necessary to explore the worker's attitude towards authority generally. The supervisor will seek to understand why the worker believes he must challenge his authority. However understanding he may be, the supervisor will still need to set reasonable limits and exert his authority to see that the work is done in accordance with agency standards.

If the supervisor's authority is exercised comfortably and consistently it can be a positive factor in enabling the worker to make use of supervision. As proposed in the earlier sections of this chapter, consistency must be coupled with flexibility and a clear recognition of individual workers' differing needs and capacities.

DECISION MAKING

Decision making always means choice. We will do this instead of that, or we will do nothing. If there were no alternatives, there would be no choice; and hence no decision could be made. Everyone makes countless decisions throughout the day, and social workers are constantly making professional decisions, sometimes very serious ones, throughout their working experience. We are concerned here with the kind of organisational decisions a team leader is required to make and the effect that his position in the hierarchy has on his role as a decision maker.

All agencies provide for certain crude divisions in decision-making responsibility. There will be certain areas in which workers usually make their own decisions, other matters that must be referred to a team leader for decision, and still other matters which the team leader must refer to higher levels for decision. The decisions a team leader must make fall into three broad, general categories: organisational, professional and personal. Decisions in any one of these categories will often require or affect decisions in the others as well.

A Review of Steps in Decision Making
Whether the decision relates to oganisational or professional matters, the steps of the decision-making process remain the same:

(1) Identify the issue requiring a decision.
(2) Identify the relevant factors which affect the decision.
(3) Consider the alternatives.
(4) Think through the consequences of acting on each alternative.
(5) Select the best alternative available.

It is important to be clear about what one is asked to decide. For the team leader there may be many relevant and sometimes conflicting factors that will affect the decision. Indeed weighing the priority of these factors involves preliminary decision making before the original issue can be.decided. Part of the skill of decision making is concerned with the realistic search for alternatives. 'Ideal' alternatives that are not really possible are no alternatives at all. The search for possible alternatives must be sufficiently thorough (and at times creative!) to assure that helpful possibilities are not overlooked, but it must not be so prolonged as to impede making any decision within a reasonable period of time. Much the same balance should be sought in thinking through the alternatives. Finally, there is the need to select the best alternative possible. Rarely is a totally satisfactory solution to be found. The decision will most often represent a compromise, and a judgement must be made as to which alternative appears to be the best answer possible within the limitations of the situation.

These are the steps in decision making. How thoroughly each step is carried out will vary with the individual temperaments of the decision makers, the importance of the decision to be made, and the time pressures for decision. Decisions must sometimes be made quickly, often on the basis of partial information, without an opportunity for as thoughtful analysis or as considered assessment as would be desirable. Particularly when he is asked to make decisions on the many matters that workers are expected to bring to a team leader for decision, the team leader may feel severely pressed. He often feels he could be much more secure in decision making if only he had more time to collect all the relevant information and time for considered assessment. If he is to use his time and energies effectively in decision making, he will need to work flexibly with individual team members of varying capabilities.

Decision Making Based on Flexible Supervision

Workers, as we have seen, must bring certain matters to the team leader for decision, and they may consult him on a variety of other matters about which decisions will need to be made. The team leader will need to clarify with each worker what sort of information he will need to make an informed decision. It is the worker's reponsibility to provide this information, either orally or in writing clearly, accurately and in whatever detail may be needed. It is the team leader's responsibility to give a prompt and well judged decision.

Two variables that are usually present when problems are brought by workers to the team leader are the capabilities of the worker and the seriousness of the problem. Within the team there may be several workers who have the knowledge, judgement and experience to make many of the decisions for themselves. They may be encouraged to consider the alternatives themselves and to make recommendations which the team leader will usually accept with little need to spend time and energy going over the same ground. With newer or less able workers, the team leader may need to review the grounds for their recommendations carefully and devote considerable time to a thorough consideration of all alternatives before making his decision.

The team leader remains accountable for the decisions he must make or approve. By 'rubber stamping' some decisions on the basis of his confidence in the worker, he will run some risk. However, by taking this risk he not only frees time and energy to spend where his efforts are most needed, but he gives additional responsibility and recognition to those workers able to carry it.

KNOWING THE WORK

Knowledge of the work being done and of the quality of that work is essential for the team leader. We have seen how this knowledge can affect the way in which the team leader carries out his decision-making duties. He has other duties, too, that must be based on such knowledge. He is to enable the worker to function effectively; he is to provide assurance to management that work has been done and assess how well it has been done; he is to note areas of unmet needs. If he is to carry out any of these duties, the team leader requires a considerable amount of information readily available to him. Case records provide one basis for obtaining this information; statistical and other reports form another; and discussion with the worker in supervisory sessions and other consultations provides a third.

It is humanly impossible for the team leader to know every detail of every aspect of the work of every member of his team. How much, then, does he need to know generally about the work? What further detail should he know in selected situations? Obviously he must know what workload each member is carrying; and this will include how many and what types of clients, groups, projects etc. the worker is responsible for, and what further duties he may have been assigned. For each case, group, project or special assignment, the team leader needs to have information available about what is to be accomplished (goals), what tasks the worker has set himself; and some estimate of the time needed to accomplish the tasks. This information can provide the basis for review and/or sampling; and the sample will indicate when further detailed information may be needed. Let us see how the team leader can use the forms of information giving that are generally provided.

Statistical and Other Reports

All agencies use a variety of statistical forms for reporting. Such information as numbers of cases, types of cases, numbers of home visits or office calls, and so on, is usually required. It is up to the team leader to become familiar with whatever forms are in use and to understand their purposes. With the advent of computers much more information can be codified and made quickly available, although some social workers resent what they see as the tyranny of computers. A computer can only give the information for which it is programmed. If the right questions are asked, if categories are set up that have meaning for the work in hand, the computer can provide quantities of useful information quickly. The team leader, with his intimate knowledge of the work involved, has a responsibility to make known to the programmers what information can be useful and to seek, himself, to understand from them the various uses to which computer information may be put.

Various experiments are currently being made in this area. Perhaps one of the most notable is the study conducted by Matilda Goldberg at the National Institute for Social Work Training and Education.[1] She has developed a single sheet form to give essential information about the work on each case which may be seen at a glance by a team leader and codified for the computer as well. Many agencies have developed their own forms along similar lines. The most usual information to be found on these forms is family composition, type of problems, some designation of the work undertaken, and the estimated length of time before the case can be closed.

If the team leader can help his workers to get such a form filled out correctly and kept up to date, this provides an excellent base for the sampling process which can lead to both more general and more detailed knowledge of the work done. It should be possible for the team leader to review all the new cases as these sheets are filled out. These in themselves give him a better idea than a simple case count of the demands on the worker. At least he can see how the worker views his tasks and the complexity or simplicity of the problems recognised. Obviously if he sees any forms where the constellation of problem, tasks and time does not make sense to him, he will wish to question the worker further. In addition, he should select a sample of cases for more extensive reading of the recording and discussion with the worker. Thus he can test with the worker the appropriateness of his planning and task recognition. If he finds evidence that the worker is not perceiving the situations accurately, it will be an indicator for a more comprehensive review of the work. Finally, the estimated time limits in this type of review sheet give the team leader cues for when to look again to see what has been accomplished.

Weekly or daily diaries provide a somewhat similar basis for review in methods such as community and residential work. However, to be equally informative about the work done they need to contain more than just a note of activity. There should be brief note of goals set and tasks accomplished at the very least.

In addition to the forms provided by the agency, team leaders sometimes devise forms for themselves. One team leader known to the author devised a very simple form which has proved invaluable to him in telling him what his team is doing and to his team in organising their work. The problem presented to him was that members of his team were frustrated because their plans could rarely be carried out. Crises and unexpected demands seemed always to be interfering with the planned work. He drew a vertical line down the centre of a piece of paper. He then drew horizontal lines making five sections, one for each day in the week. On the left of the vertical line he asked his team members to fill in their plans for each day. On the right they filled in what they actually did. They were asked to bring the form for discussion in the weekly supervisory sessions which he held with all team members. Some members were a little suspicious at first, feeling that it might be a device for checking up on them. However, it was in answer to a felt need, and they agreed to try it out. It proved most useful. As the weeks passed some 'crises' that might be anticipated or even prevented were identified. Planning became more realistic, allowing for extra demands. Individual rhythms of work were established by different team members related both to their styles of working and to the demands of their caseloads. The team leader became much more aware than he had been previously of the quantity and quality of the work being done by each team member, and he was able to use this knowledge when making assignments as well as for assessment.

Recording

Reading recording is another way of gaining knowledge of the type and quality of work being done. The usefulness of this form of communication depends greatly upon the kind of recording demanded in a given agency and the efficacy of the clerical support given to workers for this task. The team leader and team may well play a part in working out a style of recording which will usefully fit the agency's purposes and in identifying the amount of clerical support that is necessary.

Some supervisors make an effort to read all of their workers' recording in order to have a good knowledge of the work being done. The usual practice in such instances is to have the typist return the work via the supervisor who initials it before sending it on to the worker. This has the advantage of ensuring that the team leader has at least a chance to glance at any of the work he may choose, and any changes in the flow of records may alert him early to the worker who is getting behind in his recording. There are disadvantages to the system, however. The team leader may find himself devoting a disproportionate amount of his time to reading records, or the records may pile up on his desk. Probably the team leader will make decisions about how much of the recording to review in much the same way as he exercises his judgement as to how much detailed information he needs in the decision-making process. There are certainly several points at which cases and the recording in them come up automatically for review, which will give him a fair sample. These include opening and closing points, and occasions when decisions or consultation are necessary, or when there are complaints. These varied occasions generally provide a good cross-section of the total caseload.

Supervisory Sessions

It is in the regular supervisory sessions that probably the most complete understanding of the team member's work occurs. Both worker and team leader should participate in the selection of topics for discussion. The team member will want to discuss those cases, groups, projects, meetings etc. where he may be having problems and seeks consultation with his team leader. The team leader, through the review process just outlined, may have picked up certain situations about which he would like amplification or about which he sees the need for further discussion or teaching. It is as they discuss these varied matters that the team leader gets an increasingly clear picture of the work that is being done and the way in which the worker handles his assignments. This, as will be discussed in ensuing chapters, provides the base for effective work allocation and for joint participation in the teaching and learning that occurs when the team leader takes his responsibility for staff development. It also provides, together with the written material, the base for assessment of the team member's work.

EVALUATION AS A MANAGEMENT PROCESS

The team leader has a responsibility both to his workers and to management to provide an accurate and fair assessment of each person's work. Most agencies require one or more evaluations during the probationary period, and many agencies are now beginning to use some form of evaluation periodically after the probationary period has been passed. The team leader is the obvious person to provide an evaluation since his is the most intimate and informed knowledge of the work. In some agencies evaluation is officially done by the area officer, but he must still rely chiefly on the information passed to him by the team leader. If the team leader is to supply the information, he will still need to hold an evaluation session himself with the worker since evaluation is always a joint task and should only be undertaken with the full knowledge and participation of those involved.

Evaluation of Workers on Probation

The evaluation of workers on probation is, of course, crucial. It is an anxious time for the worker who may have a considerable investment in wanting to succeed in the job. It is essential to the agency that competent workers are retained, and that those who are not able to do the work satisfactorily are recognised and dismissed before they become entrenched in the post. The team leader must bend every effort to helping the worker attain the necessary skills, and in the chapters on teaching we shall discuss the varied tasks this entails. Having invested his time and energy into teaching the new worker, the team leader is naturally anxious for him to succeed. Yet at the end of the probationary period he must sit back and take a cool look at the actual achievement and make a documented recommendation as to the worker's retention or dismissal.

It is not too difficult a judgement to make in most instances. Most workers will have coped with the new experience satisfactorily, and it is clear that they should be retained. For a few, the judgement is equally simple. They have failed abysmally, and it is all too clear that they are not suited to social work. It is the borderline cases that cause the trouble. They can do some of the work, but there are difficulties. What is 'good enough'? How can one document 'potential'? The supervisor should not have to rely on his judgement alone. Well established agencies will have developed criteria for performance in this period. Sometimes the supervisor shares the teaching and evaluating task with a training division. At the very least, he should be able to consult with his immediate senior and with other team leaders in the office.

Task-centred work is a must in the probationary period. Once the supervisor has an idea of the standards to be attained, he must set appropriate tasks for the worker throughout the period. As he and the worker recognise together how the tasks have been accomplished, the basis for evaluation becomes apparent; and the final outcome should cause little surprise to either. Whether or not the agency requires more than one evaluation during the probationary period, it is useful to have an evaluation session in the middle of the period. Should the evaluation be negative at the end, there is nothing that can be done about it; but if any negatives are pinpointed at the mid-period, there is still time for the worker to try to overcome the difficulties. As far as possible the worker should know accurately what the supervisor thinks of his performance. His good work should be confirmed and the difficulties identified. Occasionally the supervisor may hesistate to express his concern for fear of overwhelming the worker or making him so self-conscious that he cannot work out the difficulties. It is indeed reasonable and requires a sensitive judgement to hold back a criticism to see if the worker can make the change on his own. However, it is not reasonable or fair to hold back one's queries for so long that the worker has no warning of what is wrong and no chance to adapt before the end of the probationary period.

When it is time to write the evaluation, the team leader should review the work and be prepared to point to evidence for any statement he may make. He should also discuss the general content of the evaluation with the worker, getting his perceptions of his performance in each area so that he may take this into account in formulating his own judgement. The final evaluation may be written out or take the form of a check sheet, depending on agency practice; but whatever it is, it should be shown to the worker and discussed so that he understands exactly what his team leader is reporting.

Periodic Evaluation
With the increasing size and complexity of most social work organisations, the need for a formal evaluation process is becoming apparent. In a small agency where the director probably has a pretty good knowledge of each worker, it may possibly be acceptable for him to have a quiet word with the team leader as to how the worker is doing and how ready he may be to take on increased responsibility. Even then justice may be seen to be done more readily if assignments, promotion, and so forth are based on written evaluations that have been discussed and read by the worker. In a large agency such a record is indispensable.

Again it is the team leader who carries the major responsibility fo assessing the work. There are two aspects of this responsibility in the management role. On the one hand, it is a succinct way of discharging accountability, of reporting that the work has been done and to what standard. On the other, it provides the information needed for deploying workers to best advantage, identifying skills, interests and potential for promotion.

The worker should be kept aware of dates of evaluation and prior to the due date the worker and team leader should review together the work that has been done since the last evaluation. In one of the regular supervisory sessions worker and team leader should agree what tasks each will need to carry out to prepare for such a review. It is, of course, far better to make such arrangements than just to start to take a worker's cases for review without any explanation, as has sometimes been done. The points to be covered in the evaluation should be known to both supervisor and worker, and each should come to an evaluation session prepared to comment on these points. The team leader will then prepare the written evaluation or check sheet and show it to the worker. As with the probationary assessment, the agency will normally provide some system of appeal should there be disagreement. Disagreement is less likely if supervisor and worker have

C

been regularly discussing together the tasks the worker has undertaken, and if they have had further opportunity to assess these tasks
together in a joint evaluation session.

In this section on assessment, we have been discussing the management aspects of evaluation. Evaluation or assessment is, of course, an
essential process in any form of teaching, and the reader is urged to review
the section on evaluation in staff development and in student supervision as well.

'PICKING UP THE PIECES'

The team leader has a responsibility to be aware of the work being
done and to take steps if he finds one of his team members falling
behind in his work. Normally, if he holds regular supervisory sessions
and reviews the work in the ways suggested in this chapter, he
should become aware of difficulties before they pile up. However, all
too frequently a team leader is called upon to take over a team that
has been without a leader for many months, and then he may find
that some workers have fallen behind.

Perhaps it says something about the importance of a team leader's
carrying out his functions that this should occur. Obviously without
a team leader a lazy or irresponsible worker may well neglect some of
his duties, but it is not only these workers who get into difficulties.
Conscientious workers may take on more work than they can possibly
handle simply because those responsible for handing out the assignments
do not realise how much they are already carrying. Other workers
may put off recording to deal more immediately with client needs until they
gradually get so far behind that the task of catching up seems insuperable.
Still others, overwhelmed with ever increasing crisis work, neglect
statutory visits or fail to close cases that they keep meaning to see
'once more' but never do because they do not have time. Without a team
leader to maintain an overview, the balance of the work is lost. Without a
team leader to help establish priorities, the work suffers and often
impossible demands stretch workers to breaking point.

Probably a first priority for any team leader taking over a long-
neglected team is to establish just what the current work load is.
Some team leaders do this by asking each worker to present a list of his
cases, specifying the problem, and stating why the case is open. Almost
invariably this sort of review results in immediately lowered caseloads
as some of the dead-wood is cleared away. The need of the team leader to
review cases to familiarise himself with the work of the team quickly
brings to light cases where recording is behind or visits unmade.
As he begins to discuss with the worker ways of remedying the
situation, the supervisor is also beginning to get to know the worker, and

they may both be feeling their way towards the most effective method of working together.

Some workers will have the tasks well in hand; others need but a little stimulus and support to get on top of the situation. There may be some who are in serious difficulties, who will need not only support but direction in order to begin to cope with the situation. The new team leader may find himself in something of a quandary. If he suggests draconian methods such as no more assignments or no field visits until the recording is finished, he immediately exposes the worker's difficulties to the rest of the team. He may try something more gradual; but if this does not work, he may well reflect that almost certainly the rest of the team is aware of the difficulty covertly if not overtly. Sometimes discussion with the whole team around problems of organisation of work may prove useful. With the worker's permission and, indeed, active participation, it may be possible to involve the team in a joint solution of the problems. Whether this is possible or not, one thing is certain. If he is to be useful to the worker, the team leader must set some limits. Setting limits, in this case, may be the most supportive thing he can do. After all, had the worker been able to set his own limits, he might not have fallen into his present situation. As ever, the team leader is faced with the challenge of engaging a worker in the recognition of what needs to be done and agreement on appropriate tasks. The team leader's task may be the more difficult because he is new to the team. He may be resented as a new broom, and the need for change may be resisted. His first tasks for himself will be to devise ways of engaging the team and each individual worker in an appropriate programme to utilise supervision effectively to enhance service to clients.

CONCLUSIONS

In this chapter we have been discussing the administrative functions of the supervisor in relation to individual workers. We have seen that his tasks include enabling workers to make effective use of supervision, decision making, providing a structure to ensure that he knows what work is being done, and assessing the work. With all these functions his practice must be flexibly focused to the individual worker's capacities, according each worker the highest possible degree of personal responsibility consistent with organisational accountability.

REFERENCE

1 E. M. Goldberg and David Truin, op. cit.

FURTHER READING

J. Algie and Clive Miller, 'Deciding Social Service Priorities', *Social Work Today*, part I, vol. 6, no. 22, part II, vol. 6, no. 23 (1976).

E. T. Ashton, 'The Application of Management Theory to the Social Services', *Social Work* (British), vol. 24, no. 2 (1967).

David Billis, 'Managing to Care', *Social Work Today*, vol. 6, no. 2 (1975).

Anne Chrichton and M. Thomas, 'Authority and the Professional Social Worker', *Case Conference*, vol. 13, nos 9 and 10 (1967).

Stephen M. Drezner, 'The Emerging Art of Decision Making', *Social Casework*, vol. 54, no. 1 (1973).

F. E. Edwards, 'Marrying Tasks to Resources', *Social Work Today*, vol. 2, no. 1 (1971).

Neville Harris and Eddie Palmer, 'A Question of Organisation', *Industrial and Community Training* (October 1975); 'Time to Plan', *Community Care* (10 September 1975).

John Hart, 'The Caseworker in the Organisation', *Social Work Today*, vol. 8, no. 41 (1977).

Robin Osmond, Roger Missing, Valerie Tunstall and Roy Lewry, 'The Caseload Monitoring System', *Social Work Today*, vol. 8, no. 16 (1977).

Ruth Popplestone, 'Staff Assessment in Family Service Units', *Social Work Today*, vol. 6, no. 7 (1975).

Josephine Rowley, 'Trial and Error', *Social Work Today*, vol. 5, no. 14 (1974).

Claudine Spencer, 'Support as a Key Problem in Social Work', *Social Work Today*, vol. 3, no. 20 (1973).

Noel Timms, *Recording in Social Work*, Routledge & Kegan Paul (1972).

Martha Urbanowski, 'Recording to Measure Effectiveness', *Social Casework*, vol. 55, no. 9 (1974).

Maurine Webley and Jef Smith, 'Information Needs of Social Services Departments', *Social Work Today*, vol. 4, no. 11 (1973).

Chapter 5

STAFF DEVELOPMENT TASKS RELATED TO INDIVIDUAL WORKERS

The teaching role of the team leader comes to the fore in relation to his responsibility for staff development. The team leader must ask himself two major questions about each team member: what does he need to know to do the job, and what does he know? The gap between what the worker knows and what he needs to know defines the area of the supervisor's teaching responsibilities. He must assess not only the learning needs but also what opportunities he can provide for learning. The first section of this chapter will be devoted to the assessment of learning needs and opportunities. The next section will discuss some of the principles and techniques involved in teaching members of staff, and finally we will examine how evaluation of staff may be used as an aid to teaching and learning.

ASSESSMENT OF LEARNING NEEDS AND OPPORTUNITIES

The team leader needs to have quite specific knowledge of what the worker needs to know on the job, what knowledge and skill the worker already brings to the task, and what can be provided in the way of learning opportunities.

What Knowledge is Needed?
No one has yet come up with a definitive statement of what knowledge is needed to do a social work job. Mention has been made already of recent research carried out variously by Goldberg, Rowbottom and Stevenson, all of whom have attempted to specify more precisely than before the tasks carried out by social workers.[1] As these and other research findings become more widely available, they should assist the team leader considerably in his task of specifying what it is a worker may need to know in order to do his job. The team leader will inevitably also call on his own experience to assess the knowledge necessary. In addition he will learn more specifically from his team members as they describe aspects of their work, problems faced and the knowledge they have brought to the situation. All of these sources

will be needed to form a proper assessment, and the team leader will find himself in a continuing process of identification of further knowledge.

From this general knowledge, he must identify what the particular worker needs to know in order to carry out his present assignment. What does he need to know today, tomorrow, this week? Everything the worker may need to know cannot be taught at once. Priorities must be set by concentrating on what must be known for immediate functioning and what knowledge is necessary as a base for further learning. For example, a new worker may need to be taught how to find his way through a case file, before he can be taught what information in it may be significant and then how to plan for his first interview with a client on the basis of the information he has found.

What Knowledge and Skill Does the Worker Bring?
If the worker is new to the supervisor, one of his first tasks will be to find out what knowledge and skills he may bring to his tasks. Usually some background information will have been given such as age, education and previous experience. From that he can deduce something of what knowledge may reasonably be expected. In the first supervisory session there is bound to be considerable mutual exploration. The team leader will want to learn about the worker and what he brings to the tasks confronting him, and the worker will want to know much the same of the team leader as well as what demands he may make. This is, of course, only the start of a continuing process, but the start may often set the pattern for future learning.

Such questions as 'Have you had much experience with old people?', or 'What do you think needs to be done in this situation?' are relevant and soon elicit some indication of the worker's knowledge. Where the worker is at a loss or indicates a lack of knowledge, the team leader may begin the teaching process by filling in immediately needed information at once. More importantly, they will identify together what may need to be learned and how to set about it. For example, a new worker may need information about the geography of the agency, the relationship of departments, the community in which he will be working, and so forth. They may agree that the team leader will take the worker round the agency immediately after the session. Manuals and organisation charts may be provided for later perusal with discussion to follow at their next meeting. As simple a plan as a walk around the district or as elaborate a plan as a series of visits with other workers may be instituted to begin the worker's familiarisation with the community in which he will be working. Already in the process of getting to know the worker, the supervisor finds himself engaged in teaching tasks.

Provision of Learning Opportunities

A central provision of learning opportunities stems from the team leader himself. The regular supervisory sessions, plus contacts in between, provide the worker with access to much information directly from his team leader, as well as providing the opportunity through discussion with the team leader to test whatever learning the worker may have been achieving from any sources. The team leader may arrange and participate in many other learning opportunities. A community worker may need to learn about certain key people in the community even though he may not be immediately involved directly with them. The team leader may well effect the introductions. Similarly a residential worker may need to know important figures in the lives of the children with whom he will be working. Again a meeting may be effected before joint work commences.

The team leader may also arrange for learning to be done through other 'teachers'. Discussion with specialist members of staff, an opportunity to observe other staff members in action, attending a meeting of the foster home selection committee before the worker has to present a case himself – all this may be arranged by the team leader. Not only does it provide an opportunity for the worker to learn from a variety of sources; but if the team leader and worker discuss the experience in a subsequent supervisory session, the learning is reinforced and confirmed. Nor should the team leader forget that much self-directed learning will be going on. Again opportunity for discussion in supervisory sessions provides a useful channel for confirmation.

Finally, of course, the major learning opportunities revolve around actual work assigned. The mechanics of assignment will be discussed in the next chapter, but it is important for the team leader to keep his worker's learning needs in mind when making assignments as well as client needs and agency needs. Let us look at two examples of how a team leader may plan a programme for learning based on work assignment.

First, carrying on with the example given previously of a very new and inexperienced worker, the learning/teaching tasks for the worker and team leader might evolve in the following fashion. The team leader and worker might agree that eventually the worker must learn to handle a varied caseload. If they are fortunate enough to work in an agency which allows a new worker gradually to build up a caseload, they can agree on what cases to try first, and next, and so on. It is the team leader's task to identify suitable cases, to make sure the worker has the necessary knowledge before he goes out on them, and to provide opportunity afterwards for discussion in a supervisory session. It is the worker's task to give proper service to the client and to provide sufficient information as to how he has done this, so that he and the supervisor can identify what he has learned and what he may still need to learn.

The worker should try to see how he can apply this knowledge in other cases and the team leader should provide assignments which will encourage him to do this. If the work is being done in an agency where it is not possible to build up the caseload in this fashion, the supervisor's task is similar but more difficult. If the worker takes over an uncovered caseload, the team leader may find himself hastily teaching whatever is necessary to help the worker deal with emergencies. This learning may be expanded and confirmed in subsequent supervisory sessions. In whatever time is left over from coping with emergencies, it becomes the supervisor's task to help the worker select which cases he may tackle in what order so that at least some of the learning may proceed in a fairly orderly fashion.

This example has been with regard to a new caseworker. In other methods the same principle holds: the supervisor should try to introduce his worker to the tasks in as orderly a fashion as is possible in the context of meeting client and agency needs. As with the caseworker, the need is to gear the demands of the assignment to the knowledge and skill that the worker already has or can achieve through preparation for the assignment. In the case of a community worker, group worker or residential worker, it is often easier than in the casework situation to provide some support for the worker while he is actually carrying out his assignments. It is more naturally accepted that the team leader or another experienced worker should be working in the same milieu as co-leader of a group, for instance, or jointly participating in a community project.

It is not only the new worker who will be interested in learning, however. The team leader has responsibility for continuing assessment of what a worker knows, what he needs to know, and what he may need to be taught. The most dramatic example of experienced workers needing to learn occurred during the Seebohm and Kilbrandon reorganisations when almost all workers had to take on what was drastically new work to them. Most workers will have some areas in which they need or wish to improve their work. Even the most highly qualified and experienced may face new learning demands as new developments occur in the field, or they themselves are engaged in action research to produce such developments. So in the second example we may consider the tasks of the team leader in using work assignments to enhance a programme of learning for the experienced worker. In this instance the worker may well have more ideas of the type of assignment he would like, and it may be a matter of the team leader's balancing learning needs and work needs in his consideration of assignments for the whole team. There will be discussion in the next chapter of how an entire team may be involved in the selection of assignments, but here we are considering how the team leader may gear individual assignments to the learning needs of an individual worker. As worker and supervisor review the ongoing work together, the supervisor may note some areas in which the worker needs to further his knowledge or skill. If they have been discussing goals and tasks together, it may well also be apparent to the worker. At any rate, once the need is identified, appropriate assignments may be sought. These should build on the skills the worker has already shown. They should allow for the use of such skills and still provide a sufficiently different demand for the worker to be able to see clearly the similarities and differences in the new work. How this may be identified will be discussed in the next section.

THE PROCESS OF TEACHING

Some basic Principles of Teaching

1. The first principle is to start where the worker is, moving from the familiar to the unfamiliar. In the example just given it was said that assignments should build on skills the worker already has. A child care worker needing to learn about work with the elderly might be given the case of an elderly person needing to move into residential accommodation. Some of the same knowledge and skills involved in moving a child into residential accommodation will be involved, yet there will be many different problems to recognise and handle. With a new worker much may be unfamiliar, but there will be some area of previous experience that will provide something familiar to grasp.

2. Movement is from the simple to the complex. This principle is not as easily attained in the field as in the classroom. Crises occurring will inevitably involve workers in complex situations before they may be fully ready for them. The team leader can make the learning a little more 'simple' by helping the worker to sort out priorities and to partialise the problem(s) that may be present. The task-centred approach is invaluable in this situation.

3. Learning is best accomplished in those situations where the learner is personally involved in doing what is to be learned. The work situation is ideal for the fulfilment of this principle. Again a task-oriented approach helps. It provides an agreed upon structure for the worker to understand what he is attempting to do.

4. Learning will be more effective if it is confirmed. The supervisor's use of regular supervisory sessions allied to the task approach means that as learning is achieved it can be discussed and reinforced or confirmed in supervisory sessions.

5. Repetition reinforces learning. Repetition may reinforce learning but it can also defeat the purpose by being boring. Repetition with a slight difference can overcome this difficulty. Fortunately few cases are exactly alike. Learning achieved with one problem family case

may be carried over to another. It will be reinforced if the worker is asked to recognise what is the same and what is different about the way in which he deals with the two cases.

Some Special Aspects of Teaching Adults
The principles of learning just listed apply generally whether one is teaching in class or field, adult or young. The team leader finds himself in a situation where he is accountable for the work that is done and has responsibility for teaching adults in order to ensure that the work is done and to certain standards. Teaching in such circumstances is attended by some problems and some advantages.

One of the advantages is that there is more known about the capabilities of the adult learner. He will already have demonstrated ability in school and perhaps in previous employment. He will have developed learning patterns and it behoves the supervisor to adapt to those patterns. Some people learn best through experience; others, by discussion or reading. Some prefer to try things out for themselves and then discuss, while others prefer explanation before action.

Usually there is considerable motivation to learn. Success on the job is dependent upon learning the skills necessary. Promotion may be dependent upon further learning. Another motivation for learning that affects most social workers is a concern for the client who, they believe, should not be put at risk through the ignorance of the worker. This same motivation can block learning upon occasion, if the worker is afraid to try something new lest it hurt the client. The team leader can provide considerable support in such a situation as he helps the worker understand the implications of what is to be tried and lends the assurance of his knowledge that it is all right to do so.

Other blocks to learning may occur. Although the fact that the worker is accountable to the team leader may provide a base and structure for learning, it may also have inhibiting effects. The worker may be fearful of exposing his ignorance to the team leader, or he may erroneously believe he is expected to act on his own initiative in situations where he has not yet the knowledge or skill to do so. We have already seen how the team leader tries to help a worker make constructive use of supervision. How well he succeeds will most certainly affect the learning possibilities. He needs the worker's participation in understanding what needs to be learned. If the worker's questions are treated with impatience or ridicule, the worker may be chary of exposing his ignorance. If the worker is made to feel stupid over a mistake, mistakes may be covered up or the worker may tend to be overly dependent upon the supervisor, checking every action beforehand to avoid further mistakes. The team leader must maintain a fine balance. Of course he should not be impatient; although being human, he will be so upon occasion. Of course he does not want to make his worker feel stupid; yet if he has made a stupid mistake, he must be made aware of it. The trick is to maintain a mutuality of involvement with each understanding the other's role in the learning and teaching tasks. With this understanding, the worker may see it as his responsibility to seek knowledge from the team leader, who in turn is responsible for providing learning opportunities for the worker. Thus rather than viewing his ignorance as a confession of failure, it is the worker's right to make it known so that together he and the team leader may devise ways in which he may increase his knowledge and skill. Similarly if the team leader really accepts that both worker and he are engaged jointly in an endeavour to increase the worker's knowledge and skill, he may the more easily and matter of factly respond to questions or point to errors as a part of their continuing work of identifying learning needs and deciding what each needs to do as a result. The questions which made him impatient may be handled by not only answering but perhaps identifying a need to work on carrying over information from one case to another. The error may indicate new goals that need to be set in the teaching tasks.

In taking on the teaching role with adults, it is essential to remain aware of the reciprocity of roles in teaching and learning. The adult brings so much to the situation. He brings many years of experience in living and working and learning. In one sense, but only in one sense, the learning may seem to thrust him back into a dependency role after years of achievement and self-direction. In so far as we are bewildered in a new situation through lack of knowledge, this is true. It is important that the team leader does not reinforce that sense of dependency but rather seeks to relieve it by making it possible for the worker to gain the necessary knowledge in a give-and-take relationship as quickly as possible. The more he can recognise what the worker does bring, the more he responds to the worker's sense of self-direction in the search for knowledge, and the more he is able to involve the worker in joint exploration of the tasks of learning, then the easier and the more effective will be the learning process.

Variations of Teaching Techniques
Probably the major teaching technique used by most team leaders is the discussion method. Some didactic teaching also occurs (that is, information giving), reading may be suggested and written work reviewed. The supervisory sessions provide a structure in which any of these methods may be used. Certainly it is in these sessions that much of the information giving occurs. Reading may be suggested in the sessions and discussed after it has been completed. Written work, mostly records and reports, can be a basis for much valuable teaching. The team leader does

not use process recording in the same way as the student supervisor, but occasionally it is possible to suggest that a worker should process an interview if a look at the interaction and the way it developed would be helpful in a particular case. More often, however, the written material will provide the suggestion for discussion rather than the detail.

It may be necessary to teach how to select significant information to go into the case record, and this material may then later form a basis for further discussion and teaching. Some agencies have clear guidelines for what goes into the record, but many do not. In either case, it is a good idea for the team leader to work out with individual workers what it is useful for them to record in relation to the teaching needs. With some workers who need little if any teaching, the minimum recording sufficient for agency accountability may be all that is required. With others who may be handling more complex cases on which they will need regular consultation, more may be required. With new workers where there may be a heavy emphasis on the teaching/learning role, it may be particularly useful to work out a concise form of recording that can be achieved within the demands of the work load and still provide easily recognised points for discussion. This is not always easily done. The form of recording will vary with the needs and abilities of the worker and may need to be changed from time to time as new areas for learning may be developed. It is worth the time spent on it, however, for in the long run it can save a great deal of time if the team leader can quickly spot learning needs and the sessions can be focused accordingly.

Another teaching technique which has been found helpful is informal role play. This, too, can be accomplished within the supervisory session. For instance, during a discussion of the worker's way of working with a client the supervisor may say, 'Let's see how this would work. You be the worker, and I'll play the client and see how it works'. Or in another case where the team leader wants the worker to understand how the client might feel, she may suggest, 'You be the client, and I'll try to play the worker as you recorded it'. This technique often has an immediacy that may be very valuable.

Use of tape-recordings may also be a useful teaching technique. The worker may, with the client's consent, tape an interview which he and the team leader can hear at leisure and discuss. This can provide much food for reflective discussion and increased understanding of how the worker is operating. Even more than process recording, this is a time-consuming exercise and so must be used sparingly, but upon occasion it may prove invaluable.

All of the techniques so far discussed have some relation to supervisory sessions. The regularity of the sessions provides a framework for establishing a certain rhythm in learning and a structure in which individual growth and development may be encouraged.

Supporting Learning

The team leader has a role in supporting learning from whatever source. Workers do a substantial amount of learning 'on their own', as it were. The team leader needs to make clear to his workers his interest in their learning from any source. They should know that he welcomes their discussion of any new learning. The very act of explaining what he has learned may clarify the worker's thoughts; and in addition the team leader may be able to extend or at least confirm the new learning.

When the team leader makes formal arrangements for someone else to teach the worker, it is again useful to discuss with the worker what has been learned. The team leader may have asked the office manager to explain certain procedures to the worker, or he may have arranged for the worker to attend an in-service training or 'away' course. A subsequent discussion of what the worker found of value in the experience will again help to clarify and confirm learning.

EVALUATION AS A TOOL FOR STAFF DEVELOPMENT

We have already discussed the team leader's role in the evaluation process from a management point of view. Evaluation may also be an invaluable aid in teaching. As he reviews the various aspects of work to be evaluated, the team leader can pinpoint what needs to be taught and what learning has already been accomplished. Both are important to learning. The sense of accomplishment provides stimulus and confidence for further learning. The recognition of what needs to be learned gives purpose and sense of direction to the learning and teaching.

The actual written evaluation is in most agencies chiefly a management document. It spells out the type and quality of practice the worker has achieved. It is in the discussions around the writing of the evaluation that its value to learning becomes apparent. This is why it is so important to involve the worker in discussion and not just present him with a written evaluation, no matter how carefully it has been prepared or how well the team leader believes he knows the worker and his practice. The process of establishing together just what they think the worker has accomplished in the period evaluated can provide new insights and understanding. As they discuss areas where improvement is needed or areas of special interest and accomplishment, they may redefine learning goals and tasks needed to achieve these goals. Particularly, perhaps, when failings have been identified, the sense of threat or loss of confidence may be lessened if there is an agreed plan as to what can be done about them.

All of this applies whether the evaluation is during the probationary period or during subsequent employment. In the previous chapter it was noted that increasingly agencies are requiring formal evaluations at regular intervals. Team leaders in agencies where this is not a requirement might well think about the advisability of setting up periodic evaluations with their workers as an aid to teaching and learning. Although a formal written evaluation may not be required by the management, a periodic review with the worker may still give an opportunity for the team leader and worker together to reassess where they are going. In their day-to-day and week-to-week contacts much may be accomplished, but they may be so concerned with individual matters that they fail to perceive the overall picture. It is good for both team leader and worker to reflect upon accomplishment as well as dealing with immediate problems. Periodic evaluation provides the opportunity.

CONCLUSIONS

In this chapter we have been concerned with some of the tasks the supervisor may need to accomplish in his teaching role. He must know what sort of knowledge and skill the work requires; he must be able to assess what knowledge and skill the worker brings; and he must provide appropriate learning opportunities. We have seen how basic principles of learning may be applied in the work situation, and discussed some of the varied teaching techniques that may be appropriate. We have seen that evaluation can be an important factor in learning and teaching. The focus throughout has been on the importance of establishing mutual involvement in the learning and teaching tasks, and on the fact that, as in other areas, worker and team leader are dependent upon each other for the success of the process.

In the next chapter we will look at the team leader's role in group learning, and the reader is advised also to refer to subsequent chapters on student supervision for further discussion of the learning process.

REFERENCE

1   See works already cited for these authors following Chapter 1.

FURTHER READING

Gemma Blech, 'Supervision', *FSU Quarterly*, (Winter 1977).
D. Burton and D. W. Barstow, 'Use of Evaluation in Staff Development', *Social Work Today*, vol. 1, no. 8 (1970).
Yona Cohn, 'The Teaching Component in Supervision', *Social Work Today*, vol. 2, no. 3 (1971).
John Haines, 'Evaluation as a Part of Supervision', *Case Conference*, vol. 13, no. 3 (1966).

Arthur L. Leader, 'Supervision and Consultation Through Observed Interviewing', *Social Casework*, vol. 49, no. 5 (1968).

Wilma Martens and Elizabeth Holmstrup, 'Problem-Oriented Recording', *Social Casework*, vol. 55, no. 4 (1974).

Chapter 6

———◆———

GROUP SUPERVISION

By the fact that he has a team, the team leader is necessarily involved in group supervision. Kadushin has clearly defined group supervision as 'the use of a group setting to implement the responsibilities of supervision. In group supervision the supervisor, given educational and administrative responsibility for the activities of a specific number of workers, meets with them as a group to discharge these responsibilities. In group supervision the agency mandate to the supervisor is implemented in the group and through the group.'[1]

A team is a formed group, a task-oriented group, composed of employees accountable to the team leader and to whom he is responsible for providing the 'services' of a team leader. The members of the group have a common interest, presumably, in the work of the agency; but most usually a team will be a fairly disparate group so far as training, experience, age and sex are concerned. The team leader must be aware of the individuals that make up his group, but he must also be aware of the team as an identity in itself, if he hopes to provide the benefits of group as well as individual supervision.

Many social workers today have some knowledge of work with groups and of group dynamics. Group workers, community workers and residential workers all work with groups during much of their working time. Caseworkers are increasingly working with groups of clients having similar interests or problems such as foster parents, patients recently returned to the community etc. It is not proposed in this chapter to discuss group work methods. In the following sections, however, some principles of group work will be discussed as they relate to the team leader's tasks with his group. Tasks related to the team will include allocation of work, provision of resources, using the team as a means of staff development, and involving the team in the administrative process. Finally, there will be a section devoted to peer group supervision and the differences between this form of supervision and group supervision.

SOME PRINCIPLES IN WORKING WITH THE TEAM AS A GROUP

It is essential to keep the purposes of the group in mind and from time to time to reassess its activities and functioning in the light of these purposes. Essentially this is a working group, and the purposes must be connected with the overall goals of the agency. There will be times when the group will function as a decision-making body and other times when it provides a means of case consultation. Much can be done to further staff development and enable the individual members to take increasing personal or group responsibility for the work. All of this can quite directly be related to agency goals of maintaining effective service to clients.

In working with the team, the team leader will use his knowledge of the individual workers, but he must also recognise that there will be significant interaction among group members. He should be aware of the sometimes shifting, sometimes constant sub-groups or diads or triads that form and of how these affect the ways in which the team may function. A team may mourn the loss of a valued member and welcome – or resent – a new member. The team leader, aware of the reaction, can influence the reception of a new member by the way in which he introduces him to the team. On the whole, the more the team may know about a member in relation to his joining the team and the more they are involved in planning for his incorporation into the team, the better. Yet the team leader must maintain reasonable balance, enabling the new member to reveal himself and his skills in appropriate ways.

As in his relations with individual workers, the team leader has a mutually responsible relationship with the team. He may ask and expect of them that they will function as professionally responsible team members, that their contributions will be towards effective rather than destructive functioning of the team, and that they will make use of opportunities the team approach offers for improving their own functioning. They may ask and expect of him that he will give the leadership that goes with his role as well as his title. As a leader he will provide opportunity for full participation by all members. He will contribute not only from his personal knowledge, but from knowledge drawn from his position in the hierarchy; and he will support the team from the advantage of this base and clarify its direction and purpose. His is the responsibility for recognising when group discussion or activity slips into meeting the more personal, as opposed to professional, needs of its members, and for bringing the focus back. He must, of course, also assess periodically with the team how well they are working towards agreed goals and be prepared to suggest new ways of working if this is necessary.

In working with a team as in working with individuals the team leader will need to maintain the same flexible but consistent approach that has been suggested in previous chapters. Problems about the use of authority, decision making and the exercise of professional responsibility and judgement may arise in relation to team functions as well as with individual workers. Teams will vary in their capacities for undertaking responsibility. Team capacity may be affected not only by the sum total of the capacities of individual members, but also by how long the team has been in existence, how well the members work together, and by many other variables. The team leader will need to know his team well and exercise considerable judgement in assessing the capacity of the team as he works out his role in relation to it. A review of some of the team leader's tasks with his team may give some ideas as to how this may be achieved.

ALLOCATION OF WORK

It is the team leader's responsibility to allocate work to his team. He may do all the work of allocation himself, or he may share this task with his team, but the responsibility for allocation remains his.

Goals for Allocation of Work

The team leader may have several goals in mind regarding the allocation of work, and some of them will be conflicting. First of all work must be assigned to get it done. Whatever work an agency accepts as its responsibility must be assigned to someone to do. Clients' needs should be considered. What sort of worker will best meet the client's needs, a man, a woman, one with special skills? Workers' needs must be considered also. What sort of cases interest the worker most? Does the case provide some aspect about which the worker needs to learn? Is worker A overloaded while worker B enjoys time for leisurely but skilled work with a very few clients? Sorting out the answers to these questions and determining priorities in allocation is a complex task. Some team leaders reserve most of the decision making in this area for themselves, others share it with their team. There are advantages and disadvantages to each method of practice, and circumstances within a given agency may well decide which is more appropriate.

The Team Leader Making the Decisions in Allocation

The team leader must, of course, know what is involved in assignments already being carried by the workers. Size of caseload is only a crude measuring device. Twenty cases because of their complexity may take all of one worker's time while twenty comparatively simple cases fill but half the time of another worker. As a result of regular supervisory sessions and structured reporting, the team leader should have a reasonably clear idea of the tasks in which the worker is involved and of the skills and interests he brings to the work. The team leader will need to allow himself time in which to review the referrals which have come for assignment so that he may make an estimate of clients' needs and the work likely to be involved in each case. Sometimes the 'match' instantly springs to mind, but the 'right' worker is not always available at the right time, nor is it always desirable to make an 'ideal match'. For instance the presenting problem may show a need for someone to work with an adolescent. The worker most skilled in the type of work is already overloaded. A competent but less skilled worker may be assigned. Or a new worker may need the experience of working with an adolescent. In this case the team leader may consider the severity of the adolescent's problem and his own availability to support the worker with possibly extra supervisory time during work on this case, as well as the worker's readiness to take on such an assignment in view of other learning demands at the same time.

Having considered the various factors, he will assign the case. In this, as in any other method of allocation, it should be open to the worker to question the assignment. On the whole, he is expected to accept the assignment unless he has some specific reason for refusal. However, there may be factors of which the team leader is unaware, and he should certainly be prepared to reconsider the assignment in the light of new knowledge. Of course the regular supervisory sessions will usually provide an opportunity for communication that gives the leader sufficient knowledge to enable him to avoid assigning against the worker's wishes, but such circumstances can inadvertently arise.

When the team leader retains responsibility for making the assignments, he is certainly fulfilling one of his duties as a team leader. He may also be saving other team members considerable time and effort which they would otherwise have to give to the process. If his allocations are made upon the basis of adequate information about the workers' present tasks and appreciation of their skills, interests and learning needs, it is an appropriate and effective method of work assignment. However, many team leaders prefer to involve the members of the team in this process for a variety of reasons.

Team Involvement in Work Allocation Decisions
It was said at the beginning of this section that whatever method of allocation he chooses, the responsibility for allocation remains with the team leader. Although it may look as if he is abrogating this responsibility to the team, in fact he may have decided that team decision is the most effective way of allocating work with this particular group. It can be seen as a way that enables workers to have responsible and professional participation in deciding what work they will undertake. It also provides workers with an opportunity to have an overview of the work of the team and some idea of what other members are doing. As referrals are discussed in the group, ideas may be exchanged as to what is diagnostically significant or what sort of work different workers see as

necessary on a case. All this provides opportunities for learning and teaching and may enrich individual members' understanding of the tasks to be handled.

With these benefits to be gained from group allocation, it may seem strange that not all team leaders use this method of allocation. There are disadvantages that in many instances outweigh the advantages. Perhaps the most serious disadvantage is that it can consume a disproportionate amount of time in relation to only a small aspect of the total work to be done. The team leader rarely saves any time for himself by this process. If he takes his responsibilities for allocation at all seriously, he must still review all referrals, and he must also arrange for the information to be disseminated to other team members. Either the referrals themselves must be passed to team members for reading, or he must prepare a digest which he may either give orally at the meeting or send in written form before the meeting. The various team members must have time to study the data if they are to make responsible suggestions regarding allocation. Depending on the number and frequency of referrals, the team may need to meet daily or once or twice a week. A team of six members and a team leader meeting for one hour equals in man-hour terms approximately one full day's work for one social worker. Experience has shown that work allocation can rarely be accomplished on the basis of one hour per week, so the time devoted to this aspect of the work may seem excessive either to administration or to workers. A worker with a demanding caseload may well wish to devote his time to his major assignment and expect his team leader to spend his time on his own responsibility for work allocation. Equally, management may query the cost effectiveness of so many man-hours devoted to allocation of work.

Other questions may be raised about the efficacy of group decision regarding allocation of work. What happens if no worker will 'offer' for a case or if two workers want the same case? How is the client's interest protected if a worker would like the case for whatever reason, but is in fact not the best worker for the case? Can a 'lazy' worker simply disregard group opinion and fail to take his full share of the load? What about the overly conscientious worker who volunteers for all the difficult or unwanted cases? A skilled team leader with a highly professional team can develop group awareness and responsibility in these areas, and the sense of responsible participation may be very rewarding for all concerned. This will take time and considerable effort. In the final analysis, the responsibility for the correct and efficient allocation of work remains the team leader's. If he chooses the team method of allocation, he must be prepared to work with his team individually and as a group so that all members can properly fulfil this obligation. He must also see to it that individual members have sufficient time to devote to this task and that time so allocated is counted in the total work assignment.

Finally, he must assure himself that the results are proportionate to the time spent and the proportion of time used is appropriate to the total assignment demands.

PROVISION OF RESOURCES

The team leader has a responsibility to his team to assure that they have the resources with which to do the work. Supplies may well be ordered through a central division of the agency, but the team leader has the responsibility for making known the needs of his team whether it be for pens or stenographic time. He needs to be aware of those items of equipment which can simplify some tasks or enable them to be done more efficiently. He needs to keep an eye on current stocks of supplies so that shortages do not occur unexpectedly.

Space, too, is a factor. As additional workers or students are added to the team, are desks being crowded together? Are there enough telephones? Is there sufficient privacy for office interviews? Are workers making home visits for sound reasons or because there is no opportunity to interview in the office?

Time, as we have seen in the chapters relating to supervision of individual workers, is a major resource. The use of time, one might say the 'gift' of time, is a vital factor in the team leader's relationship to his team. We have already seen in relation to allocation meetings how much time can be consumed in meetings. Yet the essence of group supervision is the group meeting together. Whether he calls a meeting for administrative purposes or staff development, the team leader must assess the value of the time spent in relation to the goals of the meeting. It is essential that the team members understand and agree generally with the purposes of any meetings. Workers under pressure to attend a meeting when they believe they should be attending to their clients' needs hardly make constructive participants. Meeting time must be seen to be effective and related to mutually agreed goals of work. Both meetings and individual sessions may be seen to be valid opportunities for team members and team leader to work together, each contributing from his expertise towards the overall functioning of the team.

The team leader may save time for his team, too, by his awareness of the overall scope of the team's task. How the work is divided may affect the amount of time needed to accomplish the same amount of work. In some instances a geographical division of work may prove a time saver; in others, division by certain categories or specialities meets the objective. The team leader in a residential setting has an intricate task in arranging timetables. His colleagues in the field might pick up some ideas from him as they struggle to blend effectively maximum self-determination for caseload coverage with responsibility for covering other team responsibilities such as duty days and representation on various committees and working parties.

Another resource which the team leader makes available to his team is his own general knowledge of the community or 'patch' which his team serves, plus the contacts he may have within it. Obviously this is a key role for a team leader in community work, but it is also important for team leaders in other methods. It is part of his responsibility as a team leader to know the area served, to enrich his knowledge through information shared by team members, and, in addition, to take personal responsibility for maintaining and developing contacts that will facilitate the work of the team.

STAFF DEVELOPMENT THROUGH GROUP SUPERVISION

The team leader may carry out his functions as a teacher and enabler by supplementing with group supervision the individual methods already discussed.

The Team as a Tool for Staff Development

There are many things that are better learned in a group than in an individual session. Certainly it saves time, if all or most of the team need to learn something, to provide the teaching in a group rather than going over the same content time and again in individual sessions. Learning is enriched by the opportunity for cross-fertilisation of ideas and experiences. As any teacher knows, one inevitably learns when one teaches. As members of the group take responsibility for teaching one another, they reinforce their own learning in addition to learning from one another.

One of the most common ways of using the group for teaching is to use the lecture/discussion method. Someone – it may be the team leader, a team member, or an 'expert' invited for the purpose – presents material on a subject of interest, followed by discussion by the total group. It can be a one-off meeting or there can be a series of meetings on related topics. Whoever presents the material, it is helpful for the team leader to have some idea of what will be presented and to have thought of the more important teaching points that he will want brought out and emphasised in the discussion. Either the team leader or a member of the group should be prepared to summarise at the end of the meeting so that the material and discussion are drawn together and the group is left with a clear idea of what the meeting has been about.

Another popular method of group teaching is the case consultation method. Various members of the team in turn present one of their cases for group consultation. Sometimes an outside consultant is invited to comment on the case, or sometimes the case is simply presented for comment by the group. The team leader will have to take considerable responsibility in preparation if the consultation is to be really effective as a means of staff development. In the first place he must engage the team in planning so that all know what is expected of them. It should be clear that 'consultation' is different from 'supervision'. There is an expectation that the worker will be open to new ideas and suggestions, but the responsibility for deciding whether to accept and use suggestions remains the worker's. Any 'outside expert' should also recognise this principle. The team members need to understand that a group consultation should not be used to pay off old scores, indulge in rivalries or show off. The purpose of the consultation is to explore new ways of perceiving or working with the case and to use the opportunity for widening the knowledge of all members of the team with regard to similar work. It follows that the team leader, too, will recognise that there is a difference between a possible decision-making role in a supervisory session and the role of facilitating discussion in the group consultation. He should, of course, contribute his ideas; but there is a risk that a premature, too definitive statement may cut off discussion abruptly. In preparation for case consultation, it is often useful to devote part of an individual supervisory session to helping the worker select an appropriate case and deciding what details in the presentation will be fruitful for group discussion and learning. Learning is enhanced if cases presented build one upon the other, as opposed to being selected for presentation at random.

The group may also be used to help members learn and develop by participation in a number of activities which might be termed 'learning by doing'. Role play is one such activity. Although many recently qualified workers may have taken part in role play exercises during their courses, some are more comfortable than others when participating in this activity. The team leader will need to be sensitive to the varied reactions of the team members and make some assessment of when they may feel sufficiently comfortable with one another to engage in this activity. It often helps if the team leader volunteers to play the worker (usually the most difficult and self-conscious of parts) for the first few times. Inevitably some of the player's personality is injected into any role, and the team leader will need to be alert to keep discussion to professional points and avoid personal analysis. Objectivity is strengthened if the discussants refer to names given in the role play rather than to players' own names.

Other learning by doing may involve the group in some special tasks or research. When it was first introduced, some teams carried out planned experiments in task-centred casework, for instance. Others have sought to learn more about group work, sometimes by analysing the group process in which they are engaged. Occasionally a team has agreed to form itself into a sensitivity or 'T' group for the purpose of increasing members' self-awareness and use of self in the work situation. This is a legitimate purpose, but again not all workers may be equally committed to its usefulness or wish to participate. The team leader should be aware of the need for skilled and sensitive leadership of such a group. Unless he himself, has had training in leading such groups, he should not undertake the role of leader; and indeed, even if he is trained, he may well prefer to get someone else to do it. There are elements in the role of supervisor and the role of leader of a 'T' group which can be in conflict.

The Role of the Team Leader with the Group

Much of the value of the team as a group in staff development comes from the interaction and participation of all team members. The team leader's role, then, is to stimulate and support the group participation. His is the responsibility to provide a structure in which this may happen. This requires some advance planning. There must be a suitable place for group meetings, one of the many resources for which the team leader must look. He needs to find some room which is not too large or yet so small that the group will be crowded uncomfortably. He must have ideas to present, yet encourage the group to bring out their own ideas.

Just as with individual supervisory sessions, it is a good idea to have a regular time for meetings so that all may take this into account in their planning. Also like individual sessions, it is important that all participants understand the various purposes of having meetings and have come to some agreement as to how they may be used. Some of the meetings, as we shall see in the following section, may be needed for administrative matters. However, here we are focusing on those meetings which are concerned with staff development. The team leader may suggest that there is a certain amount of time available for such meetings – possibly alternately with administrative meetings. He will then wish to explore with the group how they may use these meetings. If he has identified some appropriate areas, he may put his ideas forward; but this is best done by way of suggestion and inquiry rather than by simply presenting a programme already laid out. Members of the group may have other suggestions. Eventually a programme may be agreed. On the whole it is better not to undertake too ambitious or long term a programme. Perhaps a short series of discussion topics is planned, or the group agrees to try a round of case consultation with each member presenting once. At the end of the agreed series, the group can review what has been accomplished. The format may be continued or a new programme suggested. It allows for flexibility and variation in the meetings, and changes in the persons selected to have responsibility for leading the group.

Sometimes the team leader may undertake to plan a series of meetings and either present topics himself or get selected others to do so. At other times it may be agreed that two or three of the workers will form a small sub-committee for planning purposes. The team leader's role in the latter case becomes that of consultant or enabler, should the committee wish to confer with him. Normally the team leader tends to chair the meeting in his role of team leader; but depending on the nature of individual meetings, someone else may be leading or there may be rotating chairmen for a particular series. An essential the team leader must keep in mind regarding his role with the team as a group, rather than as individual team members, is that the group may well have needs or purposes that clash with the needs or purposes of an individual within it. He may well be aware of both because of the nature of his work with both individuals and the group. In his work with the group, group needs will come first. This is not to say he should not be aware of individual needs, and he may need to protect an individual in a situation where the group may be making him a scapegoat or attacking him. However, an individual worker may be asked to give more to the group than he gets from it, depending on his capacities and the group's needs. Some member may have occasionally to undergo a bit of boredom. The member keen for a discussion of transactional analysis may have to defer his interest while the group concerns itself with looking at simpler forms of relationship. Hopefully the alert team leader will arrange in individual sessions some outlet for the talents of those with highly specialised interests. Hopefully, too, he will find ways of involving them with the group in roles that provide satisfaction and learning to both individuals and the group. The team leader may also use individual sessions to help a team member whose understanding is below the general level of the group so that he may gain in knowledge and confidence and become a participating member as soon as possible.

The team leader has a responsibility to review and assess how the group is achieving its goals. If feedback indicates that the meetings are becoming boring, if absences are mounting, what should be done? Is the content appropriate? Are one or two members dominating discussion with their own ideas, making it difficult or impossible for others to make a contribution? Is a shift in leadership needed? What about the timing of the meetings; is the time set proving inconveninent for other work? If discussion tends to be scattered and unfocused the team leader will want to bring the group back to a sense of purpose. Towle said, 'Discussion which is not focused through direction of a leader and organized and reorganized through intermittent summarization can become flight into purposeless activity'.[2] Ultimately the group sense of frustration when this occurs is likely to undo much of the benefits of group interaction.

The team leader, whether he is leading or simply participating in meetings, takes responsibility for ensuring that the group functions effectively and that the capacities and understanding of its members are enhanced. Not every member will participate in exactly the same way or to the same degree, nor is this a desired goal. Every member should eventually get something out of the group, and each should make some contribution. A good question is as sound a contribution as an expert answer or a new idea. Discussion must inevitably sometimes bring out criticism of a team member's work or ideas. The team leader should by his example demonstrate the concept that while the comment may be rejected, the commentator is not. Team members should gain new insights into their ways of working from group discussions. What may be seen as 'evaluation' in individual sessions can be experienced as 'feedback' in group sessions. The team leader may well use the shared insights of group meetings in his subsequent sessions with workers.

THE TEAM AS AN ADMINISTRATIVE UNIT

At the beginning of this chapter Kadushin was quoted as saying that 'in group supervision the supervisor, given educational and administrative responsibility for the activities of a specific number of workers, meets with them as a group to discharge these responsibilities'. We have seen in previous chapters how the team leader discharges his administrative responsibilities in relation to individual workers and involves them in working with him in these matters. If he also involves his team as a group, he will find that his administrative tasks are easier and the functioning of the whole team is improved. The team, working on its administrative functions, obviously becomes a task-oriented group. As in all such processes there is considerable overlapping with use of the team for staff development. For instance, much learning goes on in relation to administrative tasks.

Policy Discussions
Most team leaders use group meetings for the introduction and discussion of new policy. Particularly if the team leaders are part of a management team themselves, they can bring from their own team meetings valuable information as to the anticipated or experienced results of policy. Ideally changes of policy should be proposed early enough to allow team leaders to discuss the proposed policies with their teams and bring back any questions or objections that might be raised *before* the policy is finally formulated. In reality, the team leader is often faced with the task of introducing to his workers a new policy which is to go into effect immediately. The team leader could, of course, discuss the new policy only in individual supervisory sessions;

or he could simply see to it that all his workers had whatever written material had been issued about the new policy. Policy, like law, does not really come alive until it is interpreted and implemented. Inevitably individuals will vary in their interpretation of what is meant by various phrases and of the degree to which they may believe their work will be affected. Group meetings provide an admirable structure in which to exchange ideas, come to some agreements, and (when necessary) recognise the need for further clarification before the policy is implemented.

The team's leader first priority is to become as knowledgeable about the new policy as he possibly can and to think about the implications for practice before the meeting. If the meeting is to produce thoughtful discussion, the more he can let the team members know about the policy the better. He may have to draw a fine line between allowing or encouraging ventilation of feelings and allowing the meeting to degenerate into repetitive grumbles. The focus should first be on understanding the policy and then on thinking through how it can be implemented and how this will affect service to clients. In later meetings there may be discussion on how the policy is working, and the team leader can then report success or difficulties to the policy makers.

If decisions need to be taken, the leader must be clear with the group where responsibility for decision making lies. As Wilfred Brown points out, nothing can be more destructive for a group than to come to a majority decision and then learn that it may be over-ruled by the leader.[3] If the leader is asking for the group's opinion on whatever matter, he should make it clear that he will carefully consider the opinion before making *his* decision. If, on the other hand, he is willing and able to be bound by a group decision, he should make this equally clear.

Other Tasks for the Team

As a task-oriented group, the team may undertake various administrative or management tasks. We have already seen how this may be done with regard to allocation of work. Other areas where the interaction of group ideas may be particularly helpful include such things as revision of recording or reporting requirements, organisation of the work of the team etc. As always, the team leader's responsibility is to stimulate, to provide the means of discussion, to encourage appropriate participation from all members, and to keep the focus on the tasks in hand.

PEER GROUP SUPERVISION

In peer group supervision the group takes on the responsibilities and accountability of a team leader. Individual members are accountable to the group and beyond that possibly to a director or board. The idea of peer group supervision has its attractions for some workers. There is a sense of freedom from inhibiting or binding authority and a most satisfying sense of personal and professional responsibility. As in other group experiences, there is the pleasure of contributing to others in the group. Peer group supervision can not only stimulate professional growth, but it can be seen as a confirmation of that growth. A worker's being included in such a group should indicate that he is highly qualified and able, or otherwise the question of the blind leading the blind could well arise. The benefits to each member from the contributions of several highly qualified workers may be considerable.

On the other hand, the demands on workers participating in peer group supervision are also considerable. There is inevitably far less time available for work with clients. The group must take on the administrative tasks usually done by a team leader. Certainly each participant must have high administrative skills as well as those practice skills concerned with work with clients. Time will be spent in allocation meetings. More time will be spent in a variety of meetings concerned with decision taking and reporting. Someone or everyone must maintain communications with a variety of other agencies, and sometimes representatives of those agencies may complain because they have no clear lines of contact. The danger of a higher priority being given to group needs than to client service needs can be increased as pressures mount. Some means of evaluating service and maintaining accountability to the board or director must be devised. Probably peer group supervision works best in a small agency with a group of equally experienced and well qualified workers with either similar or diversified specialities. In larger agencies the hierarchical structure militates against this type of supervision, and the administrative demands will probably be too heavy for the individual workers to carry. That the group needs to be made up of experienced, well qualified workers must again be stressed. In such a group each worker can count on the other workers for the contributions based on skill and experience that may normally be expected from a team leader. If inexperienced workers are included, they may well need more teaching time than other members can afford to give in addition to carrying service workloads and administrative responsibilities. For some workers with wide-ranging skills and interests in both direct work with clients and administration, peer group supervision provides a satisfying challenge to their well rounded professional capacities. For many others the experience of a small FSU unit is more typical.[4] The workers there responded to this challenge with enthusiasm and interest. There was heady satisfaction in proving that they could indeed carry these multiple responsibilities. After a few months, exhaustion began to rival satisfaction; and in the end they returned to a division of labour that included a unit organiser.

This book is addressed to supervisors and team leaders who in the normal course of events will rarely experience peer group supervision. Their posts are set in hierarchical structures, and they are normally employed to undertake the duties which the group takes over in peer group supervision. Nevertheless, it is important that supervisors understand the concepts of peer group supervision, what advantages it offers and what limitations there are. Within the structure of group supervision, with the team leader retaining certain tasks and responsibilities, it is possible to provide many of the advantages of peer group supervision. A team leader may work with his group in such a way as to make possible not only a significant degree of autonomy and responsibility for members qualified to use them, but also the satisfactions of contributing to other members of the group as well. In both his individual and team relationships, the team leader needs to focus the division of tasks so that the supervisor and workers support each other's work and the service of the agency is enriched and made more effective.

CONCLUSIONS

In group supervision the supervisor discharges his administrative, teaching and enabling functions through his work with the group. A combination of group and individual supervision can enrich the relationships of team members and team leader and can increase the effectiveness of their work together. The team leader must be aware of the demands he makes on his workers' time both for individual sessions and for group meetings, and assess which is the more effective method of achieving various purposes. In this chapter we have discussed various tasks the team leader must undertake in order to use the group effectively either as a vehicle for staff development or to work on administrative tasks such as allocation of work or policy implementation. We have reviewed the advantages and limitations of peer group supervision and discussed ways in which the team leader may bring to group supervision some of these advantages whilst sparing workers some of the heavy administrative demands.

REFERENCES

1 Alfred Kadushin, *Supervision in Social Work*, Columbia University Press (1976), p. 321.
2 Charlotte Towle, *The Learner in Education for the Professions: As Seen in Education for Social Work*, University of Chicago Press (1954), p. 359.
3 Wilfred Brown, *Exploration in Management*, Heinemann (1960), chapter 10.
4 Marcia Tendal and David Holder, 'Team Leadership', *FSU Quarterly*, no. 6, (Winter 1974).

FURTHER READING

Janet Dundas, 'Group Supervision', no. 12, *FSU Quarterly*, (Winter 1977).

Ruth Fizdale,'Peer Group Supervision', *Social Casework*, vol. 39, no. 8 (1958).

George S. Getzel, Jack R. Goldberg and Robert Salmon, 'Supervision in Groups as a Model for Today', *Social Casework*, vol. 52, no. 3 (1971).

Jadwiga Judd, Regina Kohn and Gerda Schulman, 'Group Supervision: A Vehicle for Professional Development', *Social Work* (US), vol. 7, no. 1 (1962).

C. Lowenstein, 'An Intake Team in Action in a Social Services Department', *The Journal of British Social Work*, vol. 4, no. 2 (1974).

Ruth Prime, 'Report on a Method of Workload Management and Weighting', *Social Work Today*, vol. 9, no. 15 (1977).

Donald Smith, 'Group Supervision: An Experience', *Social Work Today*, vol. 3, no. 8 (1972).

John Wax, 'The Pros and Cons of Group Supervision', *Social Casework*, vol. 40, no. 6 (1959).

PART THREE:
STUDENT SUPERVISION

INTRODUCTION

Part Three is concerned with the role of the supervisor in field teaching. Student supervisors in any method of social work and practising in various settings will find that the basic principles and challenges of field teaching are quite universal. The supervisor in either a probation setting or a medical setting will need to teach his student how to present the social work contribution to other professionals, be they judges or doctors. The student learning about casework, groupwork, community work or residential work, will face the responsibilities of practice in a 'live' situation. This being so, Part Three has been organised into chapters dealing with the major areas of the student supervisor's tasks relating to field work generally. (Residential workers, accustomed to comparing 'field workers' and 'residential workers', may find this nomenclature a little confusing, but 'field work' is used here in the educational terminology as compared to 'academic work'.) Some instances where methods of practice may require differential application have been noted in the following pages and illustrations have been taken from the various methods. Although the principles and challenges may be universal, each supervisor will test them in relation to his own practice knowledge based on his own setting and method of practice.

Chapter 7

◆

TASKS BEFORE THE STUDENT ARRIVES

Before a student is placed, a very considerable amount of planning and activity occurs. A suitable placement must be found, a supervisor selected. Judgements must be made that the placement will be able to meet the student's learning needs and the student will be acceptable to the placement. New supervisors will need to prepare themselves for the teaching role. Tentative plans must be established in order to ensure that the opportunities for meeting the identified learning needs are present, and so that the student may be immediately involved in learning when he does begin his placement.

BECOMING A STUDENT SUPERVISOR

Selection

Most student supervisors volunteer for assignment, although some may feel that they have been rather strenuously pressed to volunteer. Many qualified social workers see student supervision as an enrichment of the ongoing process of developing their professional skills and a logical step in professional growth and advancement. In most large organisations now, the supervisor and tutor are brought together by a training officer.

Among the training officer's duties will be that of liaising with courses and co-ordinating the provision of practical work placements. This procedure is rather more complex than in the early days of social work when tutors and supervisors often approached each other directly. Details of procedures vary from agency to agency, but in general where there is a training officer, the process includes several steps. Tutors make known to the agency how many placements they need and give the training officer some details of their expectations of the placement. At about the same time or even before, the training officer may have been circularising staff to find out who is interested in supervising students in the near future. Obviously the more details that are known in both instances the better the matching will be. The tutor will have given details about the students including what learning experiences they may need and his assessment of what kind of supervision may be appropriate for each student. The training officer relates this to the staff who are offering to take students. Is the potential supervisor experienced or inexperienced? Is his interest limited to one particular course or open to all using the agency for placements? How much time will he have available? Will he have the backing of his team leader, his area director? The training officer will be seeking information from a variety of people, tutors, prospective supervisors, those to whom the supervisor may be accountable, and so forth. To the new prospective supervisor the process may well appear as a series of hurdles to be surmounted before he can be selected.

What qualifications are sought? It is usually expected that the supervisor will hold a professional social work qualification; although as we have seen, in some developing fields the requirement may have to be waived. He can certainly be more helpful to students if he has been through a related course himself and knows something of the content taught and the demands that may be made on the student. He can hold to standards more securely if he has met those standards himself; and he can relate to new content that may be included since his student days, if he has at least had the basic teaching of a professional course.

Secondly, the expectation is that the supervisor will have demonstrated competence in practice. He need not be an outstanding practitioner, but he should be a competent one. It is crucially important that he understands and can articulate what he is doing, for he must be able to teach another rather than only demonstrate his skill. Indeed, an interest in teaching is the third qualification that is usually sought. A skilled practitioner may not always have the interest or ability to teach. In the selection process it is recognised that some prospective supervisors will not have had previous experience in teaching, but what is wanted is the interest in and the potential for teaching.

Finally, the prospective supervisor must have a reasonable expectation of having the time to supervise. If he is already stretched to full capacity by his present assignment and there can be no relief in his work load, it is unrealistic for him to take on the additional time-consuming responsibilities of a student supervisor. There must be time for weekly supervisory sessions. There must be time to read recording and to review cases for assignment. There must be time to go to supervisors' meetings and to confer with tutors when they visit the agency. Even answering day-to-day questions and being available to answer them cuts into working time. Four hours per week per student is probably the minimum time a supervisor can devote to student supervision. Weekly supervisory sessions of one to one and a half hours, time spent at meetings, reading recording, planning assignments, plus time to respond to unforeseen student needs that may occur between regular sessions – all this will take at least four to six hours a week.

Preparation of the Supervisor

Once selected, there are a number of ways in which the prospective supervisor can prepare for his new assignment. In the first place he should review his present work, looking at it from a potential student's point of view. What questions does he forsee that a student might ask? How can he explain what he is doing and, even more importantly, why is he doing it? What will he tell a student about his agency? How explain its relation to the community? What does the student need to know about the community itself? As he asks himself these questions, he may spot gaps in his knowledge. The very act of thinking through answers increases his awareness and understanding of what he is doing. Sometimes as he mentally listens to his answers he may wince as he anticipates student reaction. It is as well to identify possibly delicate, stressful or ambivalent areas ahead of time and try to think how these may be handled.

The literature on supervision is now quite extensive, and the prospective supervisor will be able to select reading from both books and articles on the subject.[1] Increasingly it has become possible to enrol for a course on student supervision before taking a student (see Part Four). In many areas such courses are given at regular intervals and are geared to the preparation of new supervisors. They are quite regularly offered by courses training for casework, and with the current focus on integrated methods are increasingly open to supervisors practising any method. If such a course is not available, the supervisor can at least usually look forward to a series of seminars for new supervisors sponsored by the course for which he is supervising.

Supervisor/Tutor Relationship

The new supervisor should expect and receive help individually from a course tutor as well. This may sometimes be difficult if the placement is geographically far removed from the course, but at least letters and the telephone may help in such circumstances. However, for the majority of supervisors, discussion with a tutor from the course will be possible.

The immediate discussion may focus on preparations for the new experience. The supervisor will need to learn from the tutor many details about the student and the course. It will be the tutor's responsibility to give information about the student that will assist the supervisor in assessing learning needs and how the student is likely to fit into the agency. Together tutor and supervisor may discuss possible teaching plans. The tutor will need to spell out the course's goals and expectations for the particular student coming to this placement, and the supervisor will need to suggest ways in which he may be able to arrange experiences to make it possible for the student to achieve these goals.

The supervisor will need to know also what he may expect from the course by way of continuing support and what is expected of him. Will the tutor be visiting the placement while the student is there? For what reason? How often? Are supervisors' meetings held and how often? What responsibility is the supervisor asked to take in regard to passing or failing a student? Courses vary in their answers to these questions to which the supervisor should be given an answer.

Most courses do arrange for tutors to visit pratical work placements. The tutor will usually visit both to assure himself that the student is indeed learning in this aspect of the course and to offer any consultation or help to the supervisor that may be appropriate. For this reason the majority of tutors visiting placements are former practitioners, many of whom have been student supervisors in the past. Sometimes tutors with only academic knowledge may be assigned to visit placements. Such a tutor may still bring considerable knowledge about the course and aspects of teaching and learning, although his understanding of the complexities of teaching in the practice setting may be more limited. However, such a non-practitioner tutor would not ordinarily be assigned to work with a new supervisor who might need more practical help and advice than an experienced supervisor.

In any event a student supervisor, either new or experienced, will usually find he is expected to develop a working relationship with tutors with whom he shares responsibility for students who are in placement. Individual supervisors and tutors will work out their relationships in different ways. Each will be contributing to the other's knowledge of how the student works and learns, and they will seek to help each other and the student to achieve a pattern of integrated academic and practice learning. New supervisors will often receive considerable help from the tutor as they develop their skills in supervision. More experienced supervisors offer considerable help to a tutor new to this aspect of his work or refreshment of practice knowledge to a tutor seeking to maintain 'touch with the field'. They may often differ in certain approaches to the work, and it will be useful to the student to realise that they can differ comfortably and yet respect each other. The tutor will need to remember that the supervisor has final authority and accountability for the work done in his agency. The supervisor must recognise that important and interesting though the practice learning may be, he should not encourage the student to cut into the requirements of academic learning in order to gain some extra experience. Sometimes the tutor may discuss a case with the student and make suggestions, but always emphasising the need to clear with the supervisor whether the suggestions are within agency policy and function. Sometimes the supervisor will provide help with reference to academic written assignments, but he will need to know what requirements the course sets for essays and other written work.

The joint goal of supervisor and tutor is to help the student make the most of his learning opportunities and each will contribute to this goal according to his capacity and setting. The student needs to be helped to see this partnership for what it is – a mutual effort to support him in learning to practise. Indeed the student is a third partner in the teaching/learning triad. Each of the three partners carries duties and obligations to the other two, not the least of which is behaviour contributing to the establishment of a climate of professional integrity in which all can operate.

SUPERVISORY·TASKS BEFORE THE STUDENT ARRIVES

Preparation of the Agency

How well the supervisor has prepared beforehand will make a considerable difference to the student's start in the agency. He should inform his colleagues and other members of the office staff that a student is coming. They should know when he is expected, how long he will be staying, where he will be located, and (at least in a general way) what he will be doing in the agency. It is sometimes puzzling to know just how much to say about a student. One is not at liberty to betray confidential information; nor should the student be made to feel that all have been discussing him and know about his affairs. Yet enough must be said for the student to come across as a person in such a way that the staff will welcome him. Certainly his name should be known, what course he comes from, and probably some indication of age and experience. After he arrives and engages in the usual office interchanges, the student may share whatever other details he wishes. Certainly the receptionist should be alerted to the date of his arrival so that she will promptly welcome him and steer him to the supervisor. Telephonists should be alerted so that they will recognise incoming calls for him from the first day.

Clients, too, may be said to be a part of the agency, and those who are going to come into contact with the student will need to be prepared. As we have seen, it is essential to prepare the residents in a residential setting. The information to be given may vary with age, sophistication and other characteristics of the residential group, but it should be such that they will have a pretty clear idea of who is coming into their midst and what he will be doing. Certainly they should know that he is a student and how long he will be staying. They should have some opportunity for discussion of their reactions, as indeed should any group into which a student is to be introduced.

In community work, too, it is very important to prepare certain key people within the community so that they may be ready to receive the student and understand what his role may be. Obviously any client, individual or group, should be prepared for the introduction of a new worker, and how this transfer is effected will depend upon the customs of the agency and what the supervisor sees as good practice. What we are considering here is the preparation of the agency which may include those clients who, particularly in the case of residential or community work, are involved intimately in the organisational structure of an agency as well as being in receipt of its services.

Casework clients tend to be more removed from the administrative functioning, and hence the preparation is more individually focused. None the less, it may be well for the supervisor at least to think about how these clients should perceive the student's role in the agency. Are they to know that the 'worker' is a student? Opinions differ on this matter, although increasingly it has come to be accepted that the student role can be interpreted to the client. Whether the student is to be known as a student or a worker, it is important that the supervisor makes sure everyone in the agency does know which it is to be. The client who calls for his 'worker' and hears the call transferred to the 'student room' may well have an adverse reaction.

It has been mentioned previously that staff should know at least in a general way what the student will be doing in the agency. Those with whom he may be working closely will need to know how much responsibility and authority a particular student is asked to carry. For instance, a young and inexperienced student may not have the resources to cope with a crisis in his supervisor's absence and may need to turn to a staff member. On the other hand, it is sometimes possible to ask a mature, experienced student to lend a hand when a crises arises in the agency and there may not be agency staff able to cope. In a residential situation, depending on the age and experience of the student, he may or may not be given authority to discipline a resident. The supervisor needs to make it clear to other staff what may be expected of the student.

The supervisor should ensure that there is adequate accommodation for the student. Many agencies now have student rooms specially equipped for the purpose, but in others there is still the problem of finding space for the student in an overcrowded office. The student does need a place he can call his own. It is not satisfactory to suggest that the student uses various workers' desks when they are out in the field or on leave. He needs a space where he may regularly hang his coat, a place where he may leave a few personal belongings such as books and papers. He needs a desk or table where he can write comfortably and with some degree of concentration. If his supervisor has an office, possibly he may share it, although this is a poor solution from both the supervisory and the student point of view. The student/supervisor relationship is a close one, and both invest it with considerable importance as they work together towards the ultimate goal of the student's successful completion of the placement. It is as well to keep some distance between them, and both will feel more comfortable if they do not constantly share the same small room.

Planning for Teaching

In addition to the preparatory office arrangements, the supervisor should be thinking about a teaching plan. It may seem premature to be considering such a plan before the student has even arrived, and in the practice setting where so many unpredictable things may be expected to occur during the placement. The plan at this stage must be tentative, and certainly it must be flexible enough to allow response to new opportunities as they occur. The length of most placements rarely exceeds a few months and may sometimes be measured in weeks (as in some residential placements). If the student is to make the most of his brief time, the supervisor must provide some structure for learning from the beginning of the placement. As the general plan evolves in the supervisor's mind, he can begin to test its feasibility even before the student arrives and avoid wasting time looking for non-existent learning opportunities later.

First, he must make some sort of tentative educational assessment on the basis of whatever information the course has provided. He will usually be told such details as the student's name, age, address, experience, educational attainments, and so forth. Opinions vary as to what should appropriately be passed on from tutor to supervisor from the information provided by references and selection interviews. While no clear-cut standards have been adopted, there is a general consensus that such information as will affect plans in relation to placement should be provided. The supervisor needs to know if the student is in a wheelchair, for instance, or if he needs a special diet when living in a residential placement. In many placements it is essential to know whether or not a student has a car available for his work. Personal details that appear to invade the student's right of privacy would not be appropriate.

The supervisor will be looking for information that will help him form some judgement of the student's capacities and interests. If he reads that the student has been a successful worker for ten years, this gives him some clue about the kind of responsibility he may be ready to take early on in the placement. If the supervisor reads that the student has been a slow learner academically and has great difficulty in writing, again there will be implications as to what he may expect from his first recording and the kind of teaching that may be needed to help him. If, after he arrives, the student demonstrates different qualities, the supervisor must be ready to revise his assessment and teaching plans accordingly.

In making this tentative assessment the supervisor looks for what the student brings to the situation. What have been his education and experience – in social work, in related fields, in life generally? How can it be used as a base for building his practical work experiences? Is there a statement about what he hopes to get from the experience? Has he requested the placement? Finally, what does the course expect he will get from the placement, and can the agency provide the requisite experience and teaching? All this must be fitted together in order to come up with a tentative teaching plan.

At this point it is obvious that the supervisor is dependent on the course for information, and unfortunately there are wide variations in the quantity and the quality of information sent. If the supervisor does not have sufficient information for intelligent assessment and pre-placement planning, he may need to request more, specifying the details he needs. As we saw in Chapter 2, for instance, not all tutors understand what information may be needed in a field in which they have not practised. It is important to know details about a student's personality if he is to be fitted into a small residential therapeutic community. A shy, reserved student going on an 'obligatory' community work placement might benefit from being assigned to work on a community study rather than being thrown into an active community centre; but only if the supervisor has been told he is shy can the judgement be made. The supervisor contemplating assigning a geriatric case would be interested to know that the student's elderly mother had died of cancer two months ago.

The supervisor will want to know where this placement fits into the student's overall learning needs. It may be the first or a subsequent placement. Presumably in no one placement is the student expected to learn 'all about social work'. The evaluation outline provided by the course gives the broad general outline of what is to be learned and provides an excellent guide for planning and teaching throughout the placement. In addition, the supervisor needs details from the tutor about what the student has learned in any previous placements and what he may be offered in future placements. A casework student may require a mixed caseload in his first placement, the ultimate goal being that he learn something about forming relationships as he begins to understand differential diagnosis. For a student already experienced in this, the goal may be to learn more about work with certain types of clients (as in adoption or work with the mentally ill) or to experiment with offering different types of work such as family therapy or time-limited work. A community work student might in one placement have learned a good deal about the skills of making a study of community needs and in another placement about implementing the findings of such a study by participation in the formation of community action groups.

Possible Early Assignments
Assuming that the supervisor does have at least a minimum of

information on which he can start planning, he will then probably start thinking in terms of early assignments. Let us look at some of the criteria for selection that may be applied in various fields of practice. One of the first tasks for students is to familiarise themselves with a new environment. They need to learn a great deal about the agency, about the staff and clients of the agency, and about the milieu in which the clients live and the agency work is done. For most students, however, the major interest centres on the kind of work that they will be expected to undertake. The first assignment, as far as possible, should include tasks that utilise previous experience, capture the student's involvement in further learning, and promise some measure of successful achievement.

Selection for a casework student at this point is relatively straight-forward. The supervisor has, theoretically at least, a number of cases from which to select one or two for early assignment; and the rest of the caseload may be built up later after he has a chance to assess the student's capabilities as demonstrated in practice. It is not always easy, however, to find just the right case or cases on which to begin. If the supervisor is looking for a new case, there is no guarantee that a suitable applicant will turn up at the right moment. It may well be wise to plan to transfer a case from a current caseload. This involves the supervisor in either reviewing his own caseload or spelling out carefully to other workers the type of case for which he is looking. This will obviously vary from student to student. For an inexperienced student almost any case may be interesting, but only some will present opportunities for an early sense of achievement. For a more experienced student, selecting a case that may be interesting will be more complicated. Should the supervisor select one of a type he has carried before? This may allow him to achieve something quickly, but on the other hand it may be threatening if, as so often happens, the student believes he is expected to perform perfectly in the area of his expertise. The student may be less self-conscious about his past experience when the case contains recognisably new elements, even though one would suppose that he would normally draw on past experience in almost any situation in which he was working with clients. If it is at all possible it is usually a good idea to have two cases available for early assignment, as the learning on one may reinforce the learning on the other. The loss or non-development of a case can be traumatic for a student if it is his only case. It is not, however, necessary to assign a full caseload at the beginning of placement. As long as the student has enough to ensure that he can start working, then the supervisor may wait and gradually increase the caseload. This allows him to gear subsequent assignments more precisely to the student's learning needs, capacities and interests as his knowledge of the student develops throughout the placement.

In group work the first assignment may not relate to a group for which the student will carry full responsibility as in the casework assignment. Here it is possible to introduce the student to practice as either a co-leader or recorder, thus assuring some support in the early stages. In such instances the supervisor may well consider the advantages and disadvantages of the student's joining a group which he himself is leading or one where another worker is the co-leader. In any event, the role of the co-leader or recorder must be clear if the student is to gain the sense of achievement mentioned earlier.

In the early days of student supervision in community work, many supervisors waited to see what choice of project might interest their students. Frequently they found that the student did not have sufficient knowledge of what was available or what the demands were to make the choice entirely on his own. Present practice is for the supervisor to select those opportunities he thinks appropriate before the student arrives and then, if there are sufficient for choice, to encourage him to observe and discuss before making a final choice of assignment.

The supervisor in community work may often not have so wide a variety of choices available to him as does the supervisor in a large casework agency. The point made earlier, that supervisors are not expected to teach 'all about social work' in any one placement has particular relevance here. The time element is another limiting factor in community work that may affect the choice of early assignments. Many of the activities in community work that are the most interesting to students are those that demand a long period of building trust and intimate knowledge between the community worker and the community. The student certainly needs to learn this, and perhaps it cannot always be done in one short placement. So the supervisor may decide that in one placement a student's first assignment needs to be to experience those processes that encourage the beginning of trust and that allow a worker to gain some knowledge of the community even though he may not remain in the placement long enough to carry through to the end results. In a different situation the supervisor might attach the student to a worker who has already completed this process so that he may have a chance to observe and perhaps even participate in subsequent developments. Either might be an appropriate early assignment so long as the teaching included helping the student to understand the total demands of the situation.

More than their colleagues in casework or group work, both community workers and residential workers have placed great importance on interviewing students before they come to the placement in order to assess how they will best fit into the groups with which they may be working. Where this is possible, it considerably eases the task of pre-placement planning, but time and distance do not always permit it. For residential placements, too, the supervisor will have to do some pre-planning and unfortunately often on the basis of inadequate information. One safeguard, as with group workers, is the possibility of making early assignments to tasks shared with more experienced workers.

CONCLUSIONS

Before the student arrives the supervisor needs to prepare in a variety of ways. During and after the selection process, he will need to prepare himself for the role of student supervisor, anticipating some of the demands and learning about student supervision from a variety of sources. He will need to plan carefully and prepare others within the agency so that the resources of the agency may be available for the student and so that the student may fit smoothly into agency functioning. Tentative teaching plans must be formulated and early assignments for the student considered. In many of these preparations the supervisor will be assisted by the student's tutor. The supervisor, tutor and student will ultimately be expected to form a working relationship in which all three seek to make the field work experience as productive as possible.

REFERENCE

1   See Bessie Kent, *Social Work Supervision in Practice*, Pergamon Press (1969), and Priscilla Young, *The Student and Supervising in Social Work Education*, Routledge & Kegan Paul (1967).

FURTHER READING

Juliet Cheetham, 'Social Work Education and the Departments of Social Work', *Social Work Today*, vol. 1, no. 12 (1971).

Adrian James, 'The Student in Social Work', *Social Work Today*, vol. 2, no. 10 (1971).

G. D. C. Woodcock, 'A Study of Beginning Supervision', *The British Journal of Psychiatric Social Work*, vol. 9, no. 2 (1967); 'Tutor, Supervisor and Student', *The British Journal of Psychiatric Social Work*, vol. 8, no. 3 (1966).

Chapter 8

TEACHING IN THE INITIAL PERIOD

The initial period of field work might well be described as the exploratory period. It is the time during which the supervisor and student meet and begin to know each other. The student begins to learn about the agency and the sorts of things that may be expected of him. The supervisor begins to have some idea of how the student responds to the demands of placement. Eventually the exploration develops into a mutual working agreement about what they will attempt together for the rest of the placement. The actual length of time for this will vary with the setting, the length of placement, and the supervisor and student who are involved; but generally a two- to four-week period is adequate for this phase.

GETTING STARTED

Pre-Placement Meeting
Very often the student and supervisor are first brought together at a meeting at the university or college. Most tutors who place their students locally try to hold such meetings. This emphasises that field work is a part of the total course and provides an opportunity for general discussion about the aims of field work. Whatever the general purposes, there is usually some chance for the supervisor to talk individually with his students. He should be prepared to answer questions about his agency and his own expectations of students. Certainly they will want a host of practical questions answered. What time should I report? How do I get there? Is parking available? There is a certain amount of self-consciousness in these encounters. Each is acutely aware that the other is sizing him up. The supervisor needs to be alert to the implications of questions. The experienced student asking knowledgeable questions about the agency may be asking for information or trying to establish himself as an experienced worker in the supervisor's eyes, or both. The inexperienced student who asks if he will see a client the first day may be either eager or fearful regarding the experience – or both. The supervisor will want to respond to the primary concern of his student. Accurate information given with a light touch can be helpful in reducing student anxiety.

If the supervisor cannot attend such a meeting, he should not only send his apologies to the tutor; he should try to reach the student directly as well. The student is placed in a difficult position if all the other students are meeting their supervisors and he is not. However well he may understand the reasons intellectually, there is some sense of rejection. Quite practically, he may have no one to talk to when all the others are busily engaged in learning about their placements. His tutor may have given him details of the placement, but he still has not met his supervisor to begin the business of getting acquainted. It helps, of course, if the supervisor can arrange to see the student at a different time, preferably before the meeting is held. If he cannot, a letter of personal welcome giving details of how to get to the placement and answering some of the usual questions will at least show the supervisor's concern and interest. Not all courses are able to hold such meetings; and sometimes, as we have seen, students meet their supervisors at the agency for a pre-placement visit.

Beginning the First Day

Whatever pre-placement meetings have been held, there remains the first day the student arrives at the agency to start his work. The supervisor needs to plan this day with some care. If at all possible, he should be there to greet the student upon his arrival. Emergencies do occur; and if the supervisor cannot be available, he should delegate someone else to look after the student with clear understanding of what this may entail.

Normally, however, the supervisor would plan to meet his student and to have his first supervisory session with him. Indeed, on this first day he may find himself having two. There is much to learn before the student may be expected to function on his own, and yet the day should not be one long supervisory session. The day should be broken up with various activities – the discussion or discussions with the supervisor, meeting people, learning the geography of the agency, learning something about the case or other first assignment.

If the supervisor has a unit of students, he must do even more planning. Usually he will hold a group meeting first to welcome them all to the agency and to cover some of the introductory things that can be covered as well or better in a group. However, he will need to schedule time for individual sessions; and this means deciding beforehand how he will order these sessions and provide activity for the others while he is seeing individual students. He may, of course, simply suggest that the students sign up for sessions with him in whatever order they wish. However, there may be reasons for assigning the times himself. It may be important to see one student first because some early activity is required by his proposed first assignment. Or the supervisor may be aware that one or more students are particularly anxious and should be seen as soon as possible. Certainly if he perceives a reason for a certain order of sessions, he should set the schedule. If no reasons spring to mind, he might as well leave it to chance and student preference.

In the opening meeting he should give the students some guidelines as to how they may employ their time whilst waiting their turn. Inevitably and rightly they may spend much of the time getting acquainted with one another, particularly if they come from different courses. Reading can be useful if it is definitely geared to some forthcoming assignment. For instance, casework students may read their pre-selected cases. Other students may be given background material regarding groups or projects with which they will be dealing. However, assigning large amounts of general reading such as agency reports and manuals is usually counter-productive, producing boredom and/or confusion until such time as the student can relate the material to actual work he may be doing in the agency. It may be a good experience for some to sit in the waiting room and observe or to explore some part of the catchment area of the agency. Whatever activities are proposed, the important thing is that the student has something related to the field work or first supervisory session to do while he waits.

The First Supervisory Session

The first session should provide a model for those to follow. The individual session provides an opportunity for student and supervisor to work together to achieve the goals of the placement. The supervisor, being the teacher, has some responsibility for giving a lead as to how this is done. From the beginning he will be seeking to involve the student in developing patterns that will be useful and agreeable to both participants. In the following report we can see an example of how one supervisor engaged the student at the start of the first session.

Miss B came in and sat down looking rather tense but expectant. I asked how the journey had been (she had been rather worried about this when I saw her at the university), and she said it had gone quite smoothly, there was plenty of time to make connections. I said I thought we might talk a little now about what it would be like in this placement, and later I would take her to see her office and meet some of the staff.

So far the supervisor has taken the lead in referring back to their previous meeting and in giving the student some idea of what will be happening.

Miss B nodded intently and continued to look expectant, so I went on to say that I'd been very interested to see she'd had a practical work experience in ―― agency (an agency similar to ours). She said yes, she'd enjoyed it very much, but she didn't expect it would be much like what she would be doing here. I said I thought the work of the two agencies was pretty much the same, but I expected she would find some difference in her role here. I wondered if she could tell me a little of what she had been doing there.

Now both supervisor and student are involved in discussion. The student is functioning well in starting to compare the placements, and the supervisor has picked up the cue and will be helping her to clarify her role in this placement.

Many things will need to be discussed in this first session. If they have not been discussed in a group meeting, domestic arrangements must be covered, such as hours of work and location of facilities. The roles of supervisor and student must be clarified. The student needs to know from the first about the supervisor's dual role of agency accountability and teaching responsibility so that he can clarify his own corresponding roles of worker and learner.

The student's first assignment should be discussed thoroughly. If he is to go out on an interview, he will need some preparation. At this stage the supervisor may have just given him the case, and the discussion may centre upon how to read the case and what to look for. On this first assignment the supervisor may well wish the student to discuss his plans with him before going out to see the client. This will, of course, vary somewhat with the experience of the student and the purpose of the interview, but usually there are benefits for both student and supervisor in such an arrangement. The student, facing new demands in an unfamiliar setting, has the security of having reviewed his proposals with someone knowledgeable and responsible. The supervisor, who only knows his student's abilities by reputation as yet, has the opportunity to assess the plans and, if necessary, to protect client, agency and student from some unwitting error. So if the assignment is made in the first session, the supervisor should make it clear to the student if he expects him to discuss the case further with him before visiting, and set a definite time to do so.

If the student's first assignment involves joint work with either his supervisor or another worker, it is equally important to discuss the plans thoroughly. The student needs to understand exactly what his role may be and what is expected of him. If his role is to observe, there will be some discussion of what may be considered significant factors. If he is to participate in the work, he will need to know what sort of role he is expected to take and what he may expect of his co-worker. In relation to any assignment, the student must know how he is expected to record and/or report.

Finally, the first supervisory session should include arrangements for the immediate future. When will supervisor and student next see each other? Arrangements will need to be made for regular supervisory sessions. They must be set not only at a time convenient to the supervisor but with due concern for the student's timetable. Particularly if the placement is only for certain days in the week, it is important to consider when the student's best time for visiting is, when he can get recording to the supervisor in advance of the supervisory sessions, and what other commitments he may have. If he is to meet with a group regularly each week, how does his supervisory session fit in, in terms of preparation or of review? In addition to the regular sessions, the student needs to know when and where he is likely to be able to find his supervisor to answer questions that may arise between sessions, and whom he should consult in his supervisor's absence.

Other Activities

Beyond the first supervisory session, the supervisor will provide other learning opportunities on the first day. A tour of the agency is useful to fix its geography in the student's mind. Some key people should be introduced. However, the supervisor should remember that too many introductions can be confusing. The first day should not be too crowded with activity. The supervisor may well plan a series of meetings during the early days of placement so that various staff members can explain their functions. On the first day it is enough to let the student know that explanations will follow. He can better remember what he has learned of importance the first day if his mind is not overwhelmed with too many impressions and too much information.

SETTLING IN

Once the student has some idea of his first assignment, the settling into work begins. In this initial period the supervisor needs to be easily accessible to his student while also maintaining the regular supervisory sessions that will hold throughout the placement. In this early part of the placement there may be many things the student needs to know before he can proceed to the next steps, and so he must come to his supervisor between sessions for answers. The supervisor should plan his own work so that during the first week or two there will be at least some time each day when the student may find him free to answer questions. Later this need will slacken off, and from the start the supervisor should help the student sort out what should wait for the regular session and what requires immediate attention.

Recording

One of the earliest demands on the student will be for recording, and it is the responsibility of the supervisor to help him to get off to a good start in this area. He needs to let the student know he may use recording both to discharge his accountability for work and to enhance his learning. He should discuss the purposes of agency recording so that the student understands not only what he is being asked to record but why. This should be immediately related to his first assignment and may be expanded later as his work covers a variety of aspects that may require special types of recording, such as court reports and foster home studies. The first essential, though, will relate to his assignment. What does the agency need to know of his activity with a case or group? Should he be keeping a diary of activity as is often the custom in residential or community work? How soon and in what form must a written report be available?

Recording for teaching purposes may take a rather different form from recording for agency requirements. This recording is primarily geared to presenting the supervisor with a picture of what the student understands has been happening. To do this the student is required to present as accurate an account as he can of the actual transactions that took place plus some analysis of the meaning. This type of recording is often called 'process recording' and is not to be confused with 'verbatim recording'. Verbatim recording is perhaps best accomplished by a skilled stenographer transcribing a tape of an interview. Process recording does not require total recall and word-for-word repetition. It does require a detailed account of the 'process' of the interaction plus analysis. It is because of the latter requirement that process recording is so useful in teaching whether or not the supervisor has been present with the student at the group meeting, interview or other transaction.

Most students welcome some structuring for their recording for supervision. It may be as simple as the threefold 'What were you trying to accomplish?', 'What happened?', 'What needs to be done next?'; or it may be a complex outline suggesting points to be noted. On the whole a relatively simple structure that allows considerable flexibility of student style of writing is probably best for first assignments. On his first assignment the student should be asked to put down in his own words within some suggested structure what happened and why he thinks it happened. In the subsequent discussion he and the supervisor can see how useful his recording is and decide if it needs to be changed in any way. For instance, if it is too sparse, the supervisor can elicit more detail through questions and then show how this could be included in the recording. If it is too detailed or confused, the supervisor may help the student to see how he might organise his material and show him where he could summarise some of the details. After all, it is important that the supervisor demonstrate by the way in which he uses the recording in individual or group supervisory sessions how it may enhance learning. In the following example we can see a supervisor using the recorded material to help the student learn in a number of ways, both about interviewing and about recording.

Miss Y's recording had presented quite a clear picture of the interview although it included little comment upon what went on. I complimented her on getting so much of the interview on paper. She flushed with pleasure but looked troubled and said she had found it a difficult interview. I said it was difficult when Mrs M thought she had solved her problem (Mrs M had borrowed money to pay the rent and had not welcomed the visit). I thought Miss Y's suggestion that she would like to talk with her to see if there was anything else the agency could do was an appropriate one considering what we knew of her circumstances. Miss Y said that Mrs M had left the television on and this had bothered her. We discussed the various reasons why clients leave the TV on – habit, a means of defence, for the children; and she decided in view of Mrs M's reluctance to let her in, it was probably defence. We discussed various ways in which she might have handled this, and then I turned back to the process record in which Miss Y had recorded a rather bald series of questions and answers. As we discussed these, I invited her to speculate on what Mrs M saw as the purpose of the questions and how she might feel about them. She quite quickly saw Mrs M's pride and that her pride was hurt by Miss Y's well meant but persistent offers of help.

The fact remains that students vary greatly in their facility with words. If a student is extremely limited in his ability to communicate in writing, the struggle to improve the quality of his writing may impede rather than enhance learning in other areas. This, obviously, would be counter-productive, and there may be times when a decision has to be made to allow the student to turn to whatever other methods of communication are possible to him, discussion, tape-recording etc. However, for most students it is indeed worth helping them to learn how to use recording not only for its enrichment of present learning, but so that they may use it in self-directing review of work in the future.

Culmination of the Initial Period

Throughout the initial period the supervisor should keep in mind the various areas in which the student will be expected to learn throughout the placement. How does he approach such areas as administration, service to clients, recording, use of supervision and other usual items in an evaluation outline? This will give clues for expectations for the future and indicate where the thrust of teaching may need to go. What lights up his interest? What does he approach reluctantly or with fear? Is he bored with some aspects? In these first days he may not have had a chance either to develop or demonstrate competence in all the various areas although he may have done in some. Whatever the supervisor can observe of either demonstrated competence or approach to the various areas will have relevance for future teaching plans and goals to be agreed.

As the initial period comes to its culmination, the supervisor should engage the student in renewed discussion of the aims and expectations of the placement. He has now had an opportunity to try himself in the agency and to learn something of the possibilities it offers. The evaluation outline can serve as a useful framework for deciding together what the educational tasks may be. It can, in a sense, be considered the syllabus of the field work course. It outlines those areas in which the student is expected to demonstrate some degree of competence. On many courses the student will have been given a copy of the outline when he first started on the course. Whether he has seen the outline or not, it becomes more immediately meaningful to him as he and his supervisor discuss the tasks that will need to be accomplished before the final evaluation is written at the end of the placement.

Not every task can be spelled out in detail at this time; and indeed if it were, the prospect might seem overwhelming to both supervisor and student. But the broad tasks can be outlined with recognition that sub-tasks will be developed along the way. The supervisor should certainly share his perception of the student's approach to the various areas covered in the outline and find out if the student agrees. Together they need to look at the expectations implicit in the evaluation outline. At the beginning of a placement the goals to be achieved by the end may seem formidable and the tasks never ending. It is important that the supervisor makes it clear that he and the student will be working together to help the student learn in the requisite areas and to reach goals. This can be demonstrated by the way they plan together in this session. They assess next steps, what they do today, tomorrow, next week. Perhaps the supervisor needs to be on the look-out for a special kind of case which will give the student the opportunity to work in a certain way. The student may be planning a next visit to a client set at a time when he may participate in family interaction or perhaps try a new way of recording following an outline suggested by the supervisor. These are immediate steps, but they must also look to the future. What can they expect by mid-placement evaluation? Here the supervisor can be helpful by pointing up the time involved in terms of how it may be used: 'In x weeks you'll have had several interviews with so and so. It needn't all be accomplished in the first interview.' Equally it is important to recognise the limitations. If two weeks of the placement have passed and the mid-placement evaluation is due in the eighth week, there are only six weeks of possibly two or three field work days in the week left, less than that when one realises that preparation for the evaluation must start before the eighth week. Supervisor and student must realise that the mid-placement evaluation can be but a signpost on the road to end of placement goals. They will wish to use it to review progress towards those goals. As they work all this out together, they will have developed a framework for the teaching and learning. As we have seen in previous chapters, the framework need not and should not be so binding as to constrict the work of either to a rigid pattern. Some structure, however, enables the work to be purposeful. The setting of goals provides an agreed point by which to measure achievement. The student is given a clear idea of what is expected and how he may set about accomplishing it. Equally the supervisor has a framework for purposeful teaching worked out in agreement with the individual student which should make his teaching the more effective.

CONCLUSIONS

The initial experiences of the student in field work will set the pattern for learning and teaching throughout the placement. The supervisor needs to anticipate the information the student will need in order to function in the early days of placement, and to provide opportunity for learning at a pace that is stimulating but not overwhelming. As the student settles in and begins to take function in the various areas of learning, he and the supervisor will need to review his approaches together. There is a need for planning teaching on the basis of an educational assessment taking into account what may reasonably be expected to be accomplished within the setting and time.

FURTHER READING

Robin Curry and Penny Gutridge, 'Student Supervison: The Step Before Reflection', *Social Work Today*, vol. 8, no. 22 (1977).

Judith C. Nelson, 'Teaching Content of Early Field Work Conferences', *Social Casework*, vol. 55, no. 3 (1974); 'Relationship Communications in Early Field Work Conferences', *Social Casework*, vol. 55, no. 4 (1974).

Chapter 9

CONTENT OF FIELD TEACHING

In this chapter we will look at what may be taught in the field, while in the next chapter we will look at various aspects of field teaching. The supervisor may choose from the rich variety of learning opportunities that the field of practice provides. Indeed, the supervisor must make choices and provide some sort of order for the learning. At the same time it is well to remember that certain aspects may arouse more enthusiasm and interest than others, and the supervisor must be sure to include content relating to all major aspects.

TEACHING BASED ON THE EVALUATION OUTLINE

As we saw in the last chapter, the evaluation outline may well be considered the syllabus of the field work course. Different methods must obviously be concerned with somewhat different knowledge and skills, and the details of various outlines reflect this. For the vast majority of such outlines these details may be subsumed under four major headings: administration, practice, recording, and use of supervision. All methods will ask for comment under these or similar headings. In addition there is often a sort of summary heading for general professional growth and development. Some courses ask for separate comments on skill shown in methods other than the major method of practice taught, while others simply include this in the practice section. Whatever the headings used, these will indicate the major areas of content of field teaching expected by the course providing the evaluation outline.

Teaching the Student to Practise in the Method of His Choice

Usually when we speak of field teaching or the practical work experience, it is this element of 'practice' that dominates. Rightly, the the most time and the most concern are devoted to it. This is what the student has come for, to learn or improve the skills of working with individuals and groups. Administration, recording, use of supervision all affect practice and will influence for good or ill his ability to learn, but it is in the area of actual practice with clients that he will be most tested and gain most satisfaction if he succeeds.

What then is involved in teaching practice? Usually it is the area of greatest security for the student supervisor. He has been a practitioner himself and knows what is involved. This is indeed an advantage as long as he avoids the danger of suggesting that the student simply follows his example rather than developing skills on the basis of his own capacities.

It is not enough simply to provide a varied assignment and then discuss how the student handles it. The supervisor must have a clear idea of what he needs to teach from the experience. In the world of practice as opposed to the academic world, he cannot always order the experiences exactly as he would wish. Cases or projects do not provide the exact cluster of teaching points he would devise were it a simulated exercise. However, if he has in mind the points he hopes to cover by the end of the placement, it will help him in selecting experience that will include at least some of the points, while he may remain alert for assignments later on to cover areas previously missed. Fortunately all of the methods have by now begun some attempts to spell out the details of what is involved in their practice, and these schemata provide a good framework from which the supervisor may pick the essential points to be taught. Unfortunately space does not permit the reproduction of a number of such schemata for the various methods, but the supervisor should make himself aware of one or more that he considers appropriate to his own method.[1] As a good broad generalisation we can say that for any method the things to be taught might be divided into three areas of knowledge, skill and awareness.

If the student is to learn to practise he will need knowledge of many things, and the field work supervisor needs to think about how much knowledge and what sort he will need to practise in his agency. For instance, he needs to learn about human behaviour. Much of this may be taught in the classroom, but the supervisor needs to think about how the student can use this knowledge in practice. The same may be said for knowledge about cultural influences, the meaning of separation, group interaction and a host of other things.

Skill may be said to be applied knowledge, how the student acts upon the basis of his knowledge. Skill develops as he practises, but it may also be taught. For instance there is a skill in asking questions. The supervisor knows what kinds of questions usually arouse trust or distrust in a client, what kind of questions pull a group together or cause it to disintegrate, or what kind of questions elicit material of value for a community study. Judgement cannot be taught, but criteria for making judgements can.

Teaching in the area of 'awareness' needs great care if it is not to slip into a therapeutic focus. It is important for the student to learn how his feelings and actions may affect his work. So long as the focus is kept on the work, the supervisor will be teaching appropriately. If a student allows a client to manipulate him because he has a need to be liked, the supervisor will need to help him to see what is happening. If the need to be liked does not appear to affect the student's work, the supervisor has no need to discuss it, and it would not be appropriate to do so.

The teaching of knowledge, skill and awareness in the placement may be taught in many ways. The supervisor may teach by discussion in supervisory sessions or meetings before the student has seen a client. Much will be done through discussion after the event, and a great deal of the learning will be accomplished by the student in the actual practice. While not all teaching revolves around the assignments, these do give the student the primary opportunity to learn, to test the learning in practice, and finally to demonstrate the knowledge and skill he has acquired.

Administration

His assignments must give the student an opportunity to learn about administration and to develop his administrative skills as well. Probably the most effective are those directly connected with his practice assignments. For instance, if a casework student is given a case on which he will have to make a request for an exception in policy, he will learn a lot more about how the agency functions than he will from merely listening to a lecture on the subject. A group work student who is given responsibility for getting authorisation for an outing, arranging financing, obtaining transport, booking accommodation etc will experience many administrative processes in accomplishing his tasks.

There is a need to teach a great deal about administration at the beginning of a placement, so that the student may function effectively within the agency. At this point both student and supervisor are well aware of the necessity, and the chief problem is to find time to cover all that is necessary. Later in the placement the teaching demands change, and sometimes the teaching slackens. This is understandable when so much interest focuses on direct work with individuals and groups, but the supervisor does have a responsibility to offer his student further learning in the administrative area. Various opportunities will arise in relation to the student's assignments. Perhaps he has a case that has been carried for many years by the agency. The supervisor can discuss the early developments with his student showing how the different policy of those days affected the decisions the worker could make. With a more recent case he might ask the student to speculate on how he would handle it if he were operating under past policies.

Cases in which there is opportunity for collaborative work not only afford the chance of teaching the practice skills in this area, but offer a rich opportunity for further study of administrative factors.

The supervisor can help the student to examine the administration of other agencies or departments and to see how this affects the work done by those with whom he is collaborating. He may also look at how members of different disciplines, such as doctors, nurses or teachers, relate to their organisational structures.

The supervisor should also consider the possibilities of involving his student in observation of administrative processes at several levels. Can arrangements be made for him to attend a board meeting, for instance? As long as his role as a student observer is made clear to members this is often possible by arrangement even if the board meetings are not generally open. Obviously if they are open to public or staff there is no problem other than arranging time, since they may be held outside the normal hours of field work. The supervisor can also be on the alert for opportunities for the student to attend other meetings of committees or working parties so that he may get the feel of how social workers contribute to the development within their agencies in a variety of ways.

Much of this comes about in the normal day-to-day working for community workers since so much of their practice is involved with committees and organising. For other methods, the supervisor may have to make special plans to ensure that his student gets an overall knowledge of administration.

Recording and Other Forms of Written Communication
Getting the student started on recording has already been discussed in the previous chapter. The student will need to continue to develop his skills throughout the placement and will need practice in the selective use of recording. As the work load increases, so does selectivity of what will be recorded for the teaching/learning process in the supervisory session. It is usually neither possible nor desirable to present all work in the form of process recording. Much may be presented in summary recording, but a particular interview or group meeting may be recorded in process whenever either student or supervisor or both wish to discuss the whole sweep of developments. At other times it may be fruitful to ask the student to record the process of an interview with someone with whom he is working collaboratively, or even a significant telephone call. In community work and residential work the usual diaries can be expanded to a process account for selected events, either with individuals or with groups, in which it is important to discuss the student's use of himself in relation to the individuals concerned.

The supervisor should review other recording periodically to assure himself that the student is adequately reporting his activities, and if necessary help him to develop a succinct style for summary recording and criteria for judging what it is important to include. In most placements there will also be an opportunity for the student to learn about correspondence and report writing. It is better to give the student guidelines about any special agency requirements (such as letters to be signed by the director instead of the writer) than to send his first efforts back for correction. The more the student can be encouraged to think about what he would get out of a letter or report if he were the recipient, the better his writing will probably be.

Use of Supervision

The most fruitful student/supervisory relationship is one responsibly worked out by both participants. However, the supervisor does have a special responsibility to offer the kind of supervision which will involve the student constructively in its use. In a sense as he enables the student to use supervision he is teaching in the content area 'use of supervision'. As we have seen, the supervisor needs to spell out carefully for the student what his expectations are regarding the use of supervision, when supervisory sessions will be held, what preparation is expected from the student, what reports he should make, what to bring for supervisory decision etc. This is only the beginning. As they continue working together the supervisor must be alert for cues in the student's response. Some students need clear limits in order to function comfortably; others welcome a more permissive atmosphere. Some like to try things out first on their own; others prefer considerable discussion before they act. It is up to the supervisor to vary his supervision flexibly (as far as he can within the limits of accountability) so that the student may make the fullest use of it. As the student develops in knowledge and competence, his use of supervision can be expected to change as the supervisor encourages qualities of initiative and independence during the placement in relation to his growing competence.

Growth of Professional Responsibility

The section 'Growth in Professional Development' is often used as a repository for comments not easily included in the other sections. It usually comes at the end of an evaluation and may be used as a sort of summary of the supervisor's impressions of the student as a professional person. What implications does this have in a discussion of planning the elements of field teaching? The supervisor's teaching does include helping the student understand professional values and ethics. There will be times in most student's practice when issues in these areas arise in relation to his work, and the supervisor will need to discuss the professional implications with the student. There are at least some values that are quite universally accepted within the profession, but the supervisor should recognise that there are others where there may be quite legitimate differences of opinion. He will make his own value system known to the student, but he should also seek to understand his student's. An often referred to example is the older supervisor who may find distasteful some of the values – and the actions following from them – that his young activist student holds. A similar situation is the young radical supervisor who is disapproving of the conformist attitudes of his mature student. Open-minded discussion in both examples can be of benefit to both supervisor and student, but neither should seek to impose his views on the other. In those cases where the differing philosophies would dictate different handling of the student's assignment, it may well be the appropriate to seek consultation with a third party, a superior within the agency or a tutor, for instance.

Teaching Multiple Methods of Practice
With growing demands for integrated practice, the supervisor may find himself asked to teach more than one method of practice. Few agencies at the time of writing yet offer opportunities for fully integrated practice either to their staff or to students. However, the supervisor of a casework student may well be asked to arrange for 'some' group work or community work experience as well. Interestingly, this does not happen so often to supervisors of other methods.

The supervisor needs to be clear with both student and tutor about what he can and cannot do. Many a caseworker has learned to work with groups on the job and developed considerable expertise. If the supervisor has a professionally qualified group worker to act as consultant, he may well take on the direct teaching or supervision himself. Otherwise he may need to look for someone within the agency who can take on the supervision of the student's work with groups. This will, of course, necessitate close co-ordination with the second supervisor and a clear spelling out of roles and accountability for the student. Whoever does the supervision, it is important to sort out how much time can be devoted to the extra assignment. Two hours a week with a group plus time for planning and recording will mean that much less time for casework assignments. If community work is the 'extra' the same considerations hold regarding the supervisor's ability to teach the subject and the time to be allotted. How many meetings will be involved, and are they held outside the usual placement hours? Can a meaningful assignment be arranged with the time available? Again, is sufficient expert consultation available to provide a good experience?

ASSIGNMENTS FOR STUDENT LEARNING

In all methods, the challenge the supervisor faces in making assignments is first how to gear them to the learning needs and capacities of his student and second, to fit them into the time available..

Assignments Geared to Learning Needs and Capacities

We have already discussed ways of identifying learning needs and capacities. This process will continue throughout the placement with corrections in perception occurring as the situation develops. It may be that a supervisor has overestimated his student's capacity at first. If he finds that his student is floundering and overwhelmed, he may need to delay further assignments until such time as the student, with his supervisor's help, can get on top of what is already assigned. However, no student should be left with only one case, with which he is having difficulty, and no chance to achieve on another case. That is why it is well to assign two cases from the beginning; but if this has not been done, the supervisor may need to think of some further assignment within the student's capacities. Generally it is not a good idea to withdraw the student from a case or other assignment, if it seems at all possible to support him through it and damage is not being done to the individual or group being served. Withdrawal exacerbates the student's feeling of failure, and he may feel also that his supervisor has no confidence in him. Usually the supervisor can help the student to partialise the situation and deal with those parts with which he can cope. If a transfer is found to be necessary, the supervisor should present the reasons to the student in terms of their joint professional responsibility for assuring a satisfactory level of service to the client. He may add the frank admission, if true, that he misjudged the case when selecting it as a suitable case for the student.

If the supervisor has underestimated the student's abilities, the matter is more easily rectified. As the placement goes on, the supervisor will need to assure himself that the work is continuing to interest and challenge the student, keeping him learning, yet not overwhelming him. Joint selection of cases, when possible, is a useful device for achieving this goal. If the supervisor has a choice of cases available he may well either describe the cases or pass the files to the student for review, and together they can decide which will be most challenging and interesting to the student.

Fitting Assignments to the Time Available

This brings us to the point of fitting assignments into the time available. The supervisor will wish to ensure that student time is used productively without either under- or overworking him. He will have a good idea of the tasks he has expected the student to undertake and this implies some estimate of the time involved. Because he keeps in close touch with the student's work he will know if new tasks have arisen or if time estimates are proving wrong. All of this should help him to keep assignments related to time available. Even so the situation may not always be what it seems. The student may appear to be fully occupied, and yet it turns out to be non-productive 'busywork'. The supervisor may assume the student can take on more because he appears to be handling everything with ease, but he does not know that the student is spending nights and weekends on placement work in addition to the regularly scheduled hours. In those settings where students keep diaries, this is less of a danger; but if no diary is kept, it may be advisable for the supervisor to inquire periodically how the student is using his time.

There is yet another aspect of the time element that may affect assignment. Many social work tasks are conducted over periods far longer than most student placements. This is true of all methods, and it poses some problems. The student needs to learn about long-term work, and so some long-term cases are transferred to him for the length of his stay, or he joins an ongoing group or project. The supervisor has the teaching task of helping him to understand what has gone before and what will be going on after he leaves. In terms of assignment, the supervisor should try to keep a balance between long-term work and assignments where the student can complete the service within the time limits of the placement.

Client Need Versus Student Need

Finally, in making assignments the supervisor is sometimes confronted with the dilemma of client need versus student need. A frequent question raised is what sort of case is suitable for a student. There can be no one answer to this. Students' previous experience and capacities vary greatly. A more pertinent question may ask how closely we can relate the level of competence needed to serve the client well to the student's level of competence. It cannot be a perfect match if the student is to be stretched and to learn. Have we the right to let someone 'learn on the client'? This can be answered by another question. Do we believe professional training is necessary? If there is no training, then it will be an unqualified worker who 'learns on the client' and often with less supervisory help available. It is an inescapable fact that someone has had to provide the first experience for every social worker, doctor, nurse or teacher now practising. So some clients will be chosen to provide learning opportunities for students. For the supervisor, the responsibility of making this choice remains. Certainly if the supervisor believes the client will be damaged, he will not assign a student. The decision must not rest only on the student's capabilities but on the supervisor's, too. The student is not alone, he will be discussing his work with the supervisor; the decision should be related to what they can accomplish together. Of course the student may make mistakes. We all make mistakes upon occasion, but few mistakes are irretrievable.

CONCLUSIONS

The content of field teaching must be carefully considered. It covers a wide range of activities related to work with clients, administration, recording, use of supervision, and professional values and ethics. The student will need to gain knowledge, skill and awareness in all these areas. The student supervisor needs to gear his continuing assignments to cover these various areas and to plan his teaching in relation to these assignments. Because he cannot provide a completely orderly sequence of learning in the live situation, it is all the more important that he work out in some detail the content he wants to cover by the end of the placement. He will then be alert to opportunities for teaching and learning as they arise and able to fit them into an integrated whole.

REFERENCE

1 See CETSWA paper no. 10, *Education and Training for Social Work* (1975), pp. 28–9, for an example.

FURTHER READING

Eleanor Hannon, 'Shared Experience: Student and Client Learn About Each Other', *Social Casework*, vol. 49, no. 3 (1968).

J. Mattinson, 'Supervising a Residential Student', *Case Conference*, vol. 14, no. 12 (1968).

Phyllida Parsloe, 'How Training May "Unfit" People', *Social Work Today*, vol. 9, no. 4 (1977).

Helen Harris Perlman, 'Believing and Doing: Values in Social Work Education', *Social Casework*, vol. 57, no. 6 (1976).

Angela Rigby, 'Residential Placements', *Social Work Today*, vol. 3, no. 11 (1972).

Chapter 10

---◆---

ASPECTS OF TEACHING IN THE FIELD

This chapter will cover a variety of the student supervisor's tasks and responsibilities in regard to teaching. Some aspects of teaching have already been covered in Part Two. These will not be duplicated here, and the reader is urged to review Chapters 5 and 6 in conjunction with the material in this chapter. The process of teaching, both individually and in groups, has been described in those chapters, a process which includes both principles and methods of teaching in the field. Certainly the same rules of learning apply; and the student supervisor may well find himself, even more than the staff supervisor, using a variety of teaching techniques. The expectation that learning will take place is universally accepted in student placements, and this expectation makes immediate demands upon the student supervisor. Because of the time-limited nature of the placement, it is all the more important to hold regular and frequent supervisory sessions. This provides the framework for learning. What the student actually does in the field is basic to his learning, but the framework of regular supervisory sessions provides both the preparation and the confirmation of learning in the field. It is also the setting for the very considerable amount of learning that goes on in the session itself. With the focus on teaching, it is possible to use these regular sessions in an inter-related pattern to develop the various areas of learning throughout the continuum of field experience.

STIMULI AND BLOCKS TO LEARNING

Stimuli to Learning
Most students want to learn. There are many self-directing students who require from the supervisor little more than guidelines to content and the standards they are expected to reach. Indeed, they will set standards for themselves often considerably higher than the expectation of the supervisor. Other students may need a push towards learning from time to time. In some instances they may not realise that there is more to be learned. Some are held back by complacency; others by the more modest assumption that they cannot achieve further. The

usual stimuli to learning will push the self-directing student along the path of learning: the supervisor may have to produce the stimuli for others.

The desire for change is a powerful stimulus for learning. The student wants to be a better worker, to try new techniques, to work with different clients or in a new setting. If he is encouraged to try new things, if he feels he has freedom to initiate, and to follow some of his own ideas, this desire for change may lead him to all kinds of learning.

Sometimes the desire for change arises out of anxiety. Nearly all students are anxious at least some of the time, and the degree of anxiety (and the student's ways of coping with it) will influence whether it may be a stimulus or a block to learning. The student may be anxious to learn so that he will not hurt clients. Or he may be anxious to learn because he knows that his assessment depends upon his demonstration that he has learned to a certain standard. This pushes him towards learning. Sometimes anxiety may be masked by apparent complacency, and the supervisor may need to point out deficiencies in order to bring the anxiety to the surface or to arouse sufficient anxiety to stimulate learning. Occasionally anxiety may be so great as to be crippling the student's efforts to learn. The supervisor will then need to discuss the anxiety with the student and help him to devise ways in which to cope with it. Reassurance is appropriate where real accomplishment can be pinpointed. A student may be helped, too, by his supervisor's firm conviction (again if realistic) that a difficulty can be overcome eventually if not at the moment. Where anxiety is impeding learning, it is important for the supervisor to devise some task on which the student may experience some accomplishment, however minute, to demonstrate to him that he can learn. There must be some pull of hope as well as the push of anxiety.

For most students in most placements there is a very considerable sense of accomplishment as they move from one task to another, and this sense of accomplishment is indeed a stimulus to further learning. There is, too, a sort of joy of learning experienced by many students. They have inquiring minds, and they like to solve puzzles and rise to challenges. Again there is a sense of accomplishment. It is important for the supervisor to be on the alert to recognise and confirm the student's accomplishments. Identifying what needs to be improved, questioning, raising appropriate anxiety are only part of the picture. Equally or more important is the recognition of good work, the confirmation to the student that his supervisor shares his sense of accomplishment.

Blocks to Learning

The supervisor needs to be aware of blocks to learning so that he may do what he can to help the student to overcome them. There are many different blocks to learning; and when set out one after the other, they present a depressing array. The supervisor or student reading this should remember that it is unlikely all the blocks will be concentrated in any single individual!

Problems with authority constitute a major obstacle to learning for some students. As we have seen there is an inescapable element of authority in supervision. The student is accountable for his work to the supervisor; ultimately the supervisor will have a considerable say in whether the student passes or fails; and the student may feel all too dependent upon his supervisor for acquiring the knowledge and skill necessary to pass. All of this is difficult enough for any student; for the student with unresolved problems about authority, it can seriously impede learning. Such a student requires a light but firm hand. Obviously the supervisor will wish to avoid any unnecessary imposition of authority that will exacerbate the student's reactions. It will not help the student if the supervisor colludes in denying the existence of his authority or fails to set reasonable limits in an effort to be 'understanding'. Some supervisors have been known to allow a student to arrive an hour or two late for weeks or to overlook failure to turn in required work because the student has 'a problem about authority'. This does not help the student to come to grips with his problem, but it does permit him to pile up trouble for himself. Most probably the supervisor will have to call on his practice knowledge in helping the student with this problem, but he must remember he is a teacher not a therapist. He and the student are jointly engaged on a project in which the student is to learn certain things required by the course within a specified period of time. It is reasonable to try to help the student to see that he is impeding his own learning, and to expect him to try to do something about it. Even though he dislikes authority, the student still has the right to expect that his supervisor will set those limits that may prevent him destroying his chances of learning.

Student learning may be blocked, as has earlier been indicated, by fear or overwhelming anxiety. These fears may take many forms. The student may be fearful of working in emotional areas with clients not only because he is fearful of hurting the client, but also because he is afraid of the emotions within himself that may be stirred up in such a situation. The former fear is probably the more easily dealt with. The supervisor can accept the student's fear of hurting the client as an extension of his concern for the client, but at the same time he can encourage the student to proceed as may be necessary. He can lend the strength of his own conviction that the proposed intervention is necessary and in the long run constructive. Since the student may be fearful that his own ineptitude may uncover something he cannot handle,

E

the supervisor can help him prepare either through extensive discussion or through role play.

The fear of the student's own emotions is often covered by an expressed concern for the client and is certainly harder to recognise. If the blockage persists, the supervisor may suspect something of the sort and explore why the student is unable to enter into this part of practice that normally one would expect to be carried out. Often the identification of the fear is sufficient to free the student to overcome it. If the problem is so deep-seated that it requires therapeutic help, the supervisor should encourage the student to seek such help, but should not attempt to provide it himself. The same holds true in those situations where the student may be handicapped by some other emotion. He may, for instance, prove unable to help parents because of some deep-seated conflict with his own parents, although he is splendid with children. It is actually very rare for this sort of crippling, deep-seated difficulty to arise. More often if there is such a blockage, it is very close to the conscious level and may be dealt with by the student himself once he becomes aware of it.

Fear of exposing ignorance or mistakes to the supervisor may also impede student learning. After all, if the supervisor does not know of the student's difficulties, he can hardly help him to overcome them. It is well, however, to recognise that a certain amount of cover-up is a perfectly healthy and inevitable student defence. If the supervisor has been able to establish the sense of partnership described earlier in the learning and teaching tasks of both student and supervisor, this particular defence is not likely to become a learning block. If the supervisor discovers that the student has been withholding difficulties, he must simply try again to help the student to understand their mutual participation. Once the student 'gives it a try' he may learn from experience that the supervisor can take his ignorance in his stride and actually help him to learn!

Personal problems may upon occasion interfere with learning. Social work students do not live in a vacuum while on a course. They fall in love; they become ill or their parents, partners or children become ill; they have accidents; they face all sorts of small or big problems; and sometimes their energies go to coping with the problems rather than learning in the field. Usually they are only too willing to discuss these problems with a sympathetic and capable person such as their supervisor. Occasionally a supervisor only knows something is wrong when he notices a falling off in the work and queries the reason. For the most part, it is appropriate to discuss these problems in a supervisory session when they affect learning in placement. Together supervisor and student may attempt to work out adjustments to relieve pressure when this is feasible. The focus is on personal counselling as it relates to the demands of placement. However, it is a danger signal to the supervisor if he finds that focus on personal counselling continues for several sessions. He will then need to assess the situation and either return the focus to field work practice or involve the tutor, with the student's consent, in a three-way assessment of what may need to be done.

Field teachers will find that there are times when the academic side of the course may seem to interrupt the learning in the field. Supervisors will recognise that as dissertations are about to become due or final examinations approach, the focus of time and energy shifts from the field temporarily. Some students who are confident of their abilities in the field but worried about the academic side may quite deliberately choose to put major emphasis on the latter. The field work supervisor may regret this if he sees learning opportunities that he would like to offer a student of great potential missed, but it is the student's decision. Supervisors learn to adjust the field demands to the regular periods of heavy academic demands such as examinations. However, if a particular student seems to be experiencing unusual pressure it may be well to consult his tutor. Sometimes adjustments can be made in the academic demands. A three-way session with tutor, supervisor and student may at least clarify the student's position and result in a more balanced division of time and energy.

Finally there is the student who just does not seem to learn and whose work provides little or no evidence of any learning. Sometimes a slow learner appears to fall into this category – he will certainly do so if the learning is so infinitesimal that he cannot pass his field work in the allotted time. For this student a referred placement may be a solution if all he needs is extra time in which to learn.

There are other students, however, whose inability to learn may not be overcome by extra time. Learning is impeded for some students by a lack of interest or ambivalence about social work. Unless their interest is aroused or their ambivalence resolved, they have little motivation to learn and indeed may find that social work is not for them. Occasionally a student finds it hard to accept some of the theories he is being asked to learn but does learn by experience in the field, thus demonstrating capacity for learning as well as ability to practice. Perhaps the most difficult to teach (fortunately only rarely encountered) is the student with a closed mind who cannot learn anything that does not fit in with some deeply held dogmatic perception. In the earlier days of social work education this was more likely to relate to religious dogma. Currently, it tends to be found among adherents of closed-system political doctrines. Many students with great faith in either a religious or a political interpretation of behaviour can learn without endangering their faiths, but the 'closed mind' student can rarely learn except possibly from another true believer. Although he may have learned little or nothing from his supervisor, it is his *performance* in the field that must ultimately be assessed. The supervisor, whose ideas may be at considerable variance with the student's, will usually welcome the participation of the tutor as they attempt to decide objectively whether or not the performance meets the standards required by the course.

TEACHING GROUPS OF STUDENTS

It is becoming increasingly rare for a student to go to an agency where he is the only student. Many agencies provide student units of varying patterns; others make a number of supervisors available, each of whom will work with one or two students as part of his assignment.

Teaching a Unit of Students

Both supervisor and students may find advantages in participating in a student unit although there are some disadvantages as well. The supervisor can concentrate on field teaching without the conflicting demands of a caseload or other responsibilities within the agency. Unit supervisors usually maintain close links with the courses that place students with them and get to know the idiosyncracies of these courses quite well. They may also have a little more time to keep up with new developments. On the other hand, they may feel somewhat isolated from the general functioning of the office and have to spend more time deliberately developing contacts, referral sources, and so forth. It may be more complicated to integrate the students into the agency and particularly to give them the feel of the administrative aspects. One great advantage of the student unit for the supervisor is that it allows him to use a mixture of individual and group supervision to enrich his teaching and the students' learning opportunities.

The student may reap the benefit of the advantages to the supervisor, and there are some specific advantages that accrue to the student, too. The support of other students in the group can be a decided advantage, as can the cross-fertilisation of ideas, particularly if students come from more than one course. However, some students feel keenly the isolation from general staff; and some prefer to have their 'own' student supervisor and not to have to compete with other students for his time and interest.

The student unit supervisor will, of course, use many of the methods of group supervision described in Chapter 6. She will find that students are generally used to group participation. Particularly for the younger ones, it is a very accepted way of working together; and they will know what is involved in group memberships and be quite open in participation. Occasionally some of the older students may be more tentative about participation or more restricted in what they consider suitable for group discussion.

One of the advantages of a student unit, the ease of communication with a group, also provides one of the hazards, a sort of contagion of alarm from time to time if one student is known to be in difficulties, or a rumour is started that 10 per cent of the class failed the last examination. If he becomes aware of something like this, the student supervisor can help by bringing it out into the open for group discussion with a more formal and balanced focus than may follow from the buzzing in the student room.

Students with Different Supervisors in One Agency

Several students assigned to one agency may have many of the advantages of a student unit or may remain quite isolated from one another, depending on the arrangements made by the supervisors involved. If the supervisors are quite separate from one another geographically in different district offices, obviously the placement becomes a 'solo' placement similar to those made for individual students in small agencies that take but one student at a time. If students and supervisors are all in one building, then if they wish, supervisors may make some effort to bring the students together for group supervision sessions as well as individual. The students may, of course, be all placed in a single room, but it is more usual for them to be sitting in a team room, which encourages more integration with agency staff. This integration is enhanced by the fact that the supervisor is also a working member of staff which gives him the advantages of involvement in administrative aspects which unit supervisors may lack. On the other hand, he may experience conflict of interest between work assignments and student supervision. Any agency worker taking one or more students for supervision should have his work load cut proportionately to the time needed for student supervision; but although accepted by administration in principle, this is still all too rarely done.

Any group supervision undertaken needs careful planning and coordination between the various supervisors involved. It is not without difficulties. Status considerations may be involved, and supervisors may have very different ideas of how they would like to use the group meetings. A natural leader may evolve or the group of supervisors may be involved in many planning meetings thrashing things out. If they take it in turn to lead the student meetings, those with less skills in group supervision may feel threatened that they will lose face in front of their students. It is sometimes difficult to find a day when all students from various courses are in placement at the same time. Particularly at the beginning, there is not as much sense of group identity as in a student group with one supervisor. It is up to the supervisors to demonstrate by their own attitudes and actions how a working group may be formed with respect for disparate interests, and group support given to individual members. The author well remembers one such group where the students were a quite supportive lot, but the supervisors were extremely competitive, each wanting to show off his or her student to best advantage whatever happened to the others! However, usually the groups can form around commonly perceived learning tasks, and as in the student units, the cross-fertilisation of ideas and the contributions of both students and supervisors may be valuable indeed.

TEACHING SPECIAL CATEGORIES OF STUDENTS

The difficulties in trying to categorise students must be apparent to anyone who supervises in social work. Yet workshops or seminars in supervision frequently have such topics as 'The problem of the older student', 'How to provide for handicapped students' etc. Recognising that any individual student will present the supervisor with a unique set of learning needs, we may still consider some generalisation which may or may not be applicable to a given student within the category.

Various Combinations of Age and Experience

The young and inexperienced student can be very satisfying to teach. He has so much to learn that the supervisor can feel reasonably secure that he has something to teach him. As the student gains in knowledge and skill, it can be most rewarding to watch his progress. This type of student is frequently assigned to new supervisors on the grounds that they should have an 'easy' first experience. However, the young student can present a considerable challenge to a supervisor and severe teaching problems. More often than other students, he may still be involved in some struggle for emancipation from his parents or have unresolved authority problems. This can affect his work in certain types of cases and his relationship with his supervisor. The young student, too, may need considerable teaching about the realities encountered in social work. Whether or not he has been brought up in a protected environment, his experience is limited; and it may be that the supervisor will need to help him to understand some of the pressures that impinge upon those he has set out to help. This is his first experience of social work; and it may be that the supervisor will also need to support him through his sense of shock when he finds that his long-held belief in his 'concern for people' is occasionally shaken by the 'people' he meets. His own sense of ineptitude may confirm his query as to the value of social work help, so that it may seem to the supervisor that he is more intent upon proving 'the system' wrong then he is upon improving his own skills in helping. The supervisor, often all too uncomfortable about the compromises he may have made himself, finds it difficult to respond appropriately to the black and white moral issues of some of the young. A grey approach seems uninspired, cynicism inappropriate and full acceptance unrealistic. Often they must agree to differ. A supervisor who demonstrates that he can respect another point of view while holding his own, and who can explain his own views with honesty and some articulateness, may free the young student to explore a variety of views and make his own choice among them. All this sounds a bit challenging, but the fact remains that most young students, whatever their views or problems, move steadily ahead in acquiring knowledge and skills in practice. They invest a great deal in helping their clients; they may have some ups and downs; but given freedom to develop and teaching that supports their efforts, they create their own effective ways of helping within a professional framework.

The older, experienced student brings many strengths to his learning experience and can be a pleasure to teach. He has already tried himself and knows that social work is what he wants to do. There will have been less guesswork in his selection, based on the kind of work he was doing. He brings knowledge gained through experience on which he and the supervisor may build. However, he too may present some challenges to the supervisor. Problems as well as benefits may spring from his experience. He has much to lose as well as to gain from coming on a course. If he fails, particularly if he fails in field work, his livelihood and his sense of worth on the job are threatened. If he encounters difficulties he may be fearful, and while most older students quietly get on with the tasks of field learning, the fear may result in either crippling anxiety or defensive assertions that there is little more he needs to learn in the field. In fact, few older students come on a course just for the qualification. They know they have things to learn, and they seriously want to learn. One of the painful things about learning for them is the realisation that they might have been more helpful to some clients in the past had they known then what they have now learned.

With the older, experienced student, the supervisor's task is to give valid recognition to the experience he brings, to help him sort out what is good and effective already in his practice, and to add to this new skills and knowledge. He must be sustained through the occasional pain of sorting out and not allowed to decry or minimise his previous accomplishments. Men and women who have held positions of responsibility and independence, whether as workers or higher in the hierarchy, may find it difficult to work out the balance of dependence/independence with a student supervisor, often a younger person and with less experience than themselves. Sometimes, in his anxiety to prove he is willing to be a 'student', the student takes an extreme position – he has has everything to learn and much to unlearn or he becomes overly conscientious and dependent. As with all students and workers, the supervisor needs to help him to work out what each may contribute to the student/supervisor relationship and what each may demand of the other to achieve their joint goals in field work. Once this is accomplished they can get on with the exciting tasks of developing new skills and interests.

The older student without previous social work experience still brings his life experiences but may be less sure in his choice of work. He has not tried himself before in socal work; and if he finds he does not like it this can be very devastating after he has already made the investment in a change of careers. Hence when difficulties occur he too may react quite strongly and will need the support of his supervisor in working them through.

In recent years, young experienced students with a year or more as a trainee or assistant social worker have become a large part of the student intake. The have decided social work is the field for them and are usually committed to training and eager for new experience and increased knowledge. They bring some already developed competence on which to build. Individually they will present some problems and difficulties for the supervisor, but as a group they provide maximum potential.

Handicapped Students

Careful planning must, of course, precede the placement of a handicapped student. Are the physical surroundings possible for the student? Are there ramps and toilet space for a wheel-chair? Are there hazards a sighted person would avoid but a blind student might run into? If the student is residential, are there special requirements regarding the height of bed or accessibility of hanging space for clothes? Can special diets be accommodated? If the condition is one in which crises may occur, are instructions available for how the supervisor may deal with it?

The supervisor needs to talk directly and matter of factly with the student about how the handicap may affect his work and how he can be of help. With a blind student, the introductory tour of the agency will obviously include much verbal description as well as time for the student to touch and feel. The supervisor should remember that once the student has memorised the physical lay-out of his office he should warn him if chairs have been moved or camping equipment dumped by the desk. The supervisor must be prepared, too, to help any handicapped student to deal with client reaction to his handicap. The student will have developed his own ways as he has met with various reactions throughout the lifetime of the handicap, and may indeed be far more aware of what is required than the supervisor. However, if the reaction of client or student affects the client/worker relationships, the supervisor's knowledge and support may be invaluable. For instance, the student who needs to prove his own independence may not recognise that his refusal of help is seen as rejection by a client. Emotionally disturbed children can be very cruel, and the supervisor may need to help the student not only to recognise the reasons for the cruelty but to assess how constructively to contain it. If the handicapped student is placed in a unit of students, the supervisor must sometimes intervene with the other students. Well meant offers of help may occasionally smother the handicapped student and deny him the chance of developing ways of coping. On the other hand, occasionally a handicapped student may unwittingly take advantage of the others as when a blind student requires time the other students can ill afford for reading to him.

Foreign Students

Many students from other countries fit into a placement very easily. Others because of colour or language difficulties are more obviously 'foreign' and may draw varied reactions from clients. Like the handicapped student, the foreign student will be experienced in coping with previously encountered reactions but may need help when these affect the working relationship. Both student and supervisor will probably be alert for obvious cultural differences. It is the almost unconscious or at least unthinking assumptions that we all make on the basis of our experience that bring occasional misunderstanding between student and supervisor or student and client. The supervisor may find himself coping with bouts of homesickness or giving practical advice about how to dress for a different climate. Occasionally the personal problems of a foreign student may be serious indeed if there are family crises or violence in the home country.

TEACHING IN BLOCK AND CONCURRENT PLACEMENTS

There are slightly different demands upon the student supervisor depending upon whether he is teaching in a block or a concurrent placement. In a block placement the student attends full time but for a shorter period of time than the same number of field work days would require on a concurrent placement. The fact that the student is there daily makes it easier for him to be integrated into the agency, and the supervisor has a wider selection of times to set for supervisory sessions or group meetings. A short total time span may provide some problems, however. Either the assignments must be appropriate to the time available, or if the student is assigned long-term cases or projects the supervisor will need to help the student to understand his role in the ongoing work. As we shall see in the next chapter, the time may be further shortened by the demands for evaluation. It usually takes about two weeks to prepare a thorough evaluation, and two weeks may involve a sizable percentage of the time in a short placement. It is important, then, that the student be given assignments in which he can demonstrate the quality of his work as early as possible. Because the student is full time, it is possible to arrange block placements at some distance from the university or college. This

F

means wider choice of placement, but it may also mean that the student and supervisor have somewhat less immediate support from the tutor if difficulties arise.

In concurrent placements the student divides his time between agency and classroom, usually going three days to one and two to the other. For the number of days required in field work, the time spread may be significantly longer than in the block placement. This allows for more flexible assignments and a more leisurely pace in working out any problems. On the other hand, the student may be handicapped by being in the field only certain days of the week. Inevitably, it seems, the most interesting clinics, the most important meeting, the most vital court is held on a classroom day, whereas assignments have to be geared to the days the student is in the field. Although occasionally a student may miss class to attend an important court or case conference, it is not to be done lightly or often. On days when the student is not in placement it usually becomes the supervisor's responsibility to deal with any crisis that may arise. He needs to do this in a way that does not take over the case from the student but rather supports the student's work. His responsible reporting to the student of his acitivity may well demonstrate this aspect of professional functioning.

CONCLUSIONS

In this chapter we have been discussing a variety of factors that may affect teaching students in the field. Students respond to a wide variety of stimuli to learning both from within themselves and from the supervisor. The supervisor must be aware of blocks as well as stimuli to learning and prepared to help the student to overcome any blocks so that learning may continue. We have also seen that different categories of students require differential teaching, while recognising that each student remains an individual with some unique learning and teaching requirements.

FURTHER READING

Elizabeth Clarkson, 'Thoughts on Supervision of Mature tudents', *Case Conference*, vol. 10, no. 6 (1963).

Hilary Davis and Paul Taylor, 'Two Agency Placements in Social Work Training', *Social Work Today*, vol. 4, no. 8 (1973).

P. M. Hammond, 'Supervision in Professional Development', *The British Journal of Psychiatric Social Work*, vol. 8, no. 2 (1965). 'Patterns of Learning in Field Work', *Case Conference*, vol. 13, no. 2 (1966).

John Harper, 'Group Supervision of Students', *Social Work* (British), vol. 26, no. 4 (1969).

K. McDougall, 'Aims and Functions of Supervision Groups', *Case Conference*, vol. 12, no. 4 (1965).

Mary Louise Somers, 'The Small Group in Learning and Teaching', in *Education for Social Work*, edited by Eileen Younghusband, George Allen & Unwin (1968).

Chapter 11

TASKS IN THE FINAL PERIOD

The supervisor has many tasks in the final period of placement in regard to evaluation, grading and helping the student to terminate his work with the agency. Evaluation or assessment is a constant through all of the student experience, but it reaches its formal culmination in the final period of placement. The evaluation process will therefore be discussed in detail in this chapter.

EVALUATION

Evaluation is an essential part of the teaching process. If learning is to be purposeful, there must be guidelines as to what is to be learned and assessment as to how, and how well, this has been achieved. Both supervisor and student make continuing assessments throughout the field work placement. Some of these remain private and personal assessments; more often they are shared in supervisory sessions and informal conversations.

In addition to the ongoing assessment, it is useful to have certain formal periods when supervisors and students take stock of the work they have been doing together. Most courses require some form of written assessment at least at the end of placement and sometimes at mid-placement as well. Some courses ask both supervisor and student to submit written evaluations; others ask for a written report only from the supervisor. Whoever does the writing, it is essential, as with so much else in the supervisory process, that the evaluation should be the result of a real and mutual involvement by the two persons concerned in the task of assessment.

For both individuals involved, the recognition of the importance of assessment usually brings with it a variety of emotional responses. Inescapably it is connected with grading. Indeed a grade, even if limited to 'pass' or 'fail', is but the shorthand for the measurement of achievement that is spelled out in detail in the written evaluation. No wonder, then, that there is concern expressed by supervisors and anxious inquiry by students as to what will be assessed and how judgements as to achievement should be formed.

Each course works out its own criteria of what should be assessed, based on those factors it deems important to the practice of social work. Often the supervisor finds himself involved, together with tutors and sometimes student representatives as well, in working out what these factors should be. In actual fact they are making decisions about what should be taught in field work. The student can only be evaluated upon what he has been taught and/or had an opportunity to demonstrate in his practice. Evaluation outlines will vary according to the differing objectives of methods and of courses. Political skills may warrant a detailed section in a community work outline, yet be scarcely mentioned in a casework evaluation. Ability to get along with colleagues is surely important in all forms of social work, but its effect on every aspect of the work may be more clearly seen in residential work and hence given more emphasis in residential assessment. There are two essential elements in deciding what areas of performance should be evaluated: they must be important to practice and clearly recognisable to both students and supervisors as valid objectives of the teaching/learning process.

The second area of concern, how judgements should be formed, involves both standards and evidence. This is an area in which the supervisor should expect – and demand – considerable guidance from the course for which he may be supervising. It is fair neither to the student nor to the supervisor to expect him to judge the student solely by his own individual standards. Frequently courses convene groups of tutors, supervisors and students to work on guidelines both for standards and for the evidence required to establish how a student is meeting those standards. This applies as well in determining the varying levels of performance. The supervisor may find himself participating in such a group or at least reaping the reward of such a group's consensus on these points. In addition, many courses make consultation available to supervisors at times of evaluation or grading. New supervisors, particularly, should feel free to request such consultation even if it is not routinely provided to all supervisors.

The evaluation *process* itself, however, is the major responsibility of the supervisor with his student. This process involves preparation for the evaluation, an evaluation session, the writing of the evaluation and the continued use of the evaluation.

Preparation for Evaluation
Usually the student will have had some preparation for evaluation from his course. The tutors will have explained that evaluation is a part of field work learning, and he may have been given a copy of the evaluation outline which his course uses. If the supervisor has used the evaluation outline with the student earlier in discussing the aims of the placement, this will have increased his familiarity with it. Again, if the supervisor

has held the sort of semi-formal discussion described in Chapter 8 in assessing how he takes hold in the beginning, he will already have had some introduction to the process. None the less, when the first written evaluation looms, there is apt to be some apprehension; and the supervisor will probably need to help the student understand what he may anticipate and how to prepare for his part in the process.

First of all, the supervisor should again clarify with the student the purposes of the evaluation and share his interpretation with the student. There are two purposes: to judge the student's work and progress, and to ensure that his educational needs are being met. The first of these purposes may be said to reflect the administrative function. It is a report that describes the assignments the student has undertaken and the quality of his work on them. It is a formal statement provided to the educational authorities to show whether or not the student has fulfilled the requirements of the course. The second purpose remains educationally focused. As the extent and quality of the work are identified the strengths and weaknesses of the student are shown, so that it becomes clear in what areas further teaching is needed. The evaluation provides the base both for confirming what has been accomplished and for pointing to the direction of further accomplishment.

Once the student understands these purposes, he has some focus for his own analysis of how he has used the placement. Courses vary considerably in the amount of participation that is expected of the student, but in recent years the trend has been towards more rather than less participation. Some courses require the student to write a full self-evaluation. Others expect him to prepare some part of the written evaluation, such as a description of his learning experiences, which may include the types of assignments with which he has dealt and the variety of skills he has attempted to use in working on them. Still other courses see the written evaluation as solely the responsibility of the supervisor but expect that it will be based on a full and free discussion with the student. It is the supervisor's responsibility in all these different situations to be clear with the student about what he is expected to do and to help him set about his preparations. The supervisor should make sure that the student has a copy of the evaluation outline or whatever guidelines are provided, and that he has some picture of what the subsequent evaluation discussion session will be like. If the student is to write in advance, it is particularly important for the supervisor to make clear what the general standards of performance for students are at this point in the placement. Self-evaluation can be a painful experience, particularly if the student has unrealistically high expectations of himself. Most students approach evaluation with some anxiety, and many tend to project high demands from their supervisors. This leads them to exaggerate their faults and sometimes neglect their strengths. The supervisor needs to help the student to see that he is asked to give a balanced account of himself and to judge himself by realistic standards. It helps to achieve that balance if the supervisor reviews the generally accepted standards and expectations with him.

In preparing himself for the evaluation session, the supervisor will need to review the work of the student throughout the period covered by the evaluation. Although the supervisor's concern is with the quality of his work now, it is important to review where he started from and what happened along the way. With the size of most student assignments it is often quite feasible to re-read recorded work from the beginning. The supervisor will also want to look at any notes he may have made following supervisory sessions during the period. If the student has worked with other staff members, either collaboratively or by being directly accountable to them, he will want to consult with them. There is as yet no consensus on the best way to handle written evaluations when more than one supervisory person has been involved in a significant part of the learning experience. However, the supervisor himself usually has the closest connection with the course from which the student comes; he has the clearest idea of the standards expected; so it may be considered his responsibility to evaluate the comments and observations of others in the light of that knowledge and to incorporate this assessment into his overall evaluation of the student perfomance.

The Process of an Evaluation Session

The structure of such a session will vary with the setting and the styles of the individuals involved. Usually it is like any other supervisory session except that the focus is more surely and directly on evaluation. Care should be taken to ensure privacy and guard against interruption, and sufficient time should be set aside so that all the necessary points may be discussed. Some supervisors start by looking at the objectives or tasks that were agreed at the beginning of placement. Others like to follow the points on the evaluation outline, and still others ask the student where he would like to start. In the latter case, the student almost invariably starts with an area of some difficulty, possibly out of anxiety to get the worst over.

Discussion should cover all of the areas that will be covered in the written evaluation. It is a chance for both supervisor and student to test their thinking about the student's performance in discussion with each other. Any evaluative comment should be backed by evidence. It is not enough to say, 'I think you are showing increased ability to handle hostility'; but rather, 'Since your first interview with Mrs H when you were floored by her anger you've come a long way, as shown by the way you handled the interview with Mr Z last week'. If the supervisor suggests that the student is a poor time-keeper, again the evidence should support the statement. One or two occasional lapses early in the placement do not warrant such a categorisation, but habitual lateness does.

If there is no real evidence, but the supervisor has a strong feeling that there is something of concern in the student's work, he may question the student about it in the evaluation session, labelling it clearly as a guess. 'I can't put my finger on it, but I have a feeling that you . . .' opens the area up for discussion. The student may confirm the feeling, in which case they may properly discuss how this affects his performance and comment may later go into the written evaluation. However, if the student denies what is suggested and the supervisor has nothing to back his intuition the matter should be dropped unless further evidence comes out later.

The content of discussion will, of course, vary with the type of placement and course. It should focus on the various tasks the student has undertaken, and it should be seen as a part of a continuing process. Thus the supervisor and student will look back together on the objectives and tasks they discussed early in the placement. They will discuss the student's current achievements in relation to these, and they will look forward to what is to be done next. If this is a mid-placement evaluation, they will be planning what each may do to help the student achieve further learning during the rest of the placement. Particularly if an area of weakness has been identified, it is important for the student's morale as well as a stimulus for further learning to identify what can be done about it. Equally, in areas of special aptitude or interest, it is important to explore what avenues there may be for further development. If it is a final evaluation there may still be discussion of what the student may be able to do in his next placement or job.

The Written Evaluation

Writing a clear, succinct, fair evaluation is an acquired skill, and many supervisors find it a difficult task. Usually the course provides an outline, but occasionally only rough notes of what is to be discussed are given. Whether the supervisor orders the structure himself or follows an outline, some clear progression and separation of topics should be present. Even following an outline the supervisor may find it difficult to do this. For instance, since 'recording' reflects casework, one often finds comments on the student's casework skills included in remarks that are designed to focus on his ability to record.

There is a need to comment on a variety of factors and to substantiate the comment, yet the evaluation must not be too voluminous. If there is a section where either the student or the supervisor has given summarised details of the assignment, it helps to refer to the assignments on which the comment is based: 'Mr Young showed his ability to sort out complex factors in his assessment of both the D and M cases; or

Miss Smith's ability to keep her head in a crisis was demonstrated when Y attempted to take over the tenants' group meeting'.

These comments say something about aspects of the student's performance and make reference to the assignments on which they are based. They do not detail all the complex factors which faced Mr Young, nor do they attempt a full account of the meeting in which a takeover was attempted. The details of the validation remain on record in the agency files, and the agreement of supervisor and student to cite these particular examples provides evidence without unduly lengthening the document.

The supervisor faces many challenges in trying to describe the student's performance in words that will have a clear meaning to others. For instance, one cannot just say that a student is improving. From what level of performance has he improved? Reference to a previous evaluation or brief description of his former level is needed. 'Frequently' may be once a week or daily. It is usually not enough simply to say that a student is 'interested in administrative aspects' or 'able to accept agency function and structure'. How does he show his interest? Does he raise appropriate questions regarding agency structure and function? The following example shows the sort of detail which brings a vivid picture of the student's approach.

This was Mrs A's first social agency experience other than Probation. She was immediately intrigued in sorting out the likenesses and contrasts between the clientele and operation of two such dissimilar settings, raising intelligent questions based on her observations and review of agency written material. She experienced the usual initial discomfort at moving from the more structured setting with its inherent authority component and built-in work deadlines to a relatively unstructured voluntary agency serving a primarily non-delinquent population. However, she was soon able to make the necessary adjustment and has had no difficulty working with agency function, structure and procedures. She has fitted well into both the formal and informal relationship and communication networks. She is a well accepted and actively participating member of the large student group and is equally accepted and respected by agency professional and clerical staff.

It has sometimes been said critically that an evaluation of a student says as much about the supervisor and the agency as it does about the student. Actually a good evaluation should say quite a bit about the supervisor and agency so that it is clear how any judgements were formed. The student's ability to learn must be related to what opportunities for learning and practice have been offered. The supervisor reveals his interpretation of standards and expectations when he is commenting on how well the student has met these.

Perhaps nowhere does the supervisor feel as self-conscious and vulnerable as when writing comments on the use of supervision. If the student has not made good use of supervision, has the supervisor been sufficiently skilful and flexible in offering a type of supervision with which the student can engage? Many supervisors worry about this aspect; but the need is, as always, to try to present the situation as accurately and with as much balance as possible. A brief description of what was offered and how it was received is a valid way of documenting the comment, particularly since it is open to the student to disagree with the description if he sees it differently. One able and experienced community work supervisor offered this pen picture: 'H is so critical of himself that I found myself unable to offer further criticism, but rather attempted to understand this and offer advice on ways round it so that he could function effectively.' Later she wrote, 'When we established that he felt very vulnerable, had high ideals and expectations for himself which his skills did not match up to, we got along more comfortably'. The student thoroughly agreed with both statements and the student/supervisor relationship was enhanced rather than threatened by the evaluation.

It is an ethical principle that nothing must be added to the written evaluation once the student has read and signed it. The evaluation stands as the supervisor's report as to how the student has fulfilled his responsibilities to learn and practise in the placement, and as their joint assessment of learning accomplished and learning yet to be achieved.

Use That May Be Made of the Evaluation

Once the evaluation is written, the student should have an opportunity to read it at leisure and discuss it further with his field work supervisor. Memories of an oral discussion sometimes vary, and it is important that both supervisor and student have a chance to agree on what results from the evaluation session. The supervisor may well be willing to make changes in the written evaluation if the student persuades him that his memory is faulty or that he has misinterpreted what the student said. On the other hand, upon occasion the supervisor may wish to say something about the student with which the student disagrees. In this case the student must have some opportunity to register his disagreement. Sometimes the supervisor will write in the evaluation, 'The student disagrees with me but . . .'. Or he may offer the student the opportunity to attach a statement to the document giving his objections.

When the written evaluation is sent to the university or college this should not mean the end of its use to student and supervisor. If it has been a mid-placement evaluation, it should most certainly be used throughout the rest of the placement as a guide and reference for further learning. Normally, a copy of the first placement evaluation is sent to the second placement supervisor. He will use it as a base for planning before the student arrives, and it may also provide a base for discussion in early sessions. It is useful if the student can also have a copy of the evaluation. Some courses do not give the student a copy, fearing that it may contravene regulations about the 'return of examinable material' or that the student may in some way misuse the copy. This seems a bit unfair; for if the second placement supervisor has a copy to which he may refer, it seems advisable that the student should also have a copy to refresh his memory.

GRADING

Grading, or the decision that the student has passed or failed, is in a sense the culmination of the assessment process. Courses vary in their grading procedures; but whatever the procedures the supervisor, as the person with the most intimate knowledge of the student's field work, plays a vital role. Grading in field work can be difficult. Whether it is desirable or not is a matter of some controversy. Some courses opt for a pass/fail system on the grounds that it is difficult to achieve objective grading in situations that may or may not be clearly comparable. If they also use pass/fail for academic subjects, this seems a reasonable solution. If, however, they distinguish between levels of work in some aspects of the student's academic performance, then it seems illogical that they do not do so in the vitally important subject of the student's ability to practise.

If the supervisor is required to participate in grading, he will need a considerable knowledge of the varied levels of student performance. His own experience, often limited to one student at a time, cannot fully equip him in this area; but, hopefully, group discussions of supervisors and tutors plus past records kept by the course will be of assistance. Students are asked to do different things in different placements and have different ranges of learning opportunities available to them. How, then, may their performance be compared? It is here that a task-centred approach is invaluable. A student in community work may have the task of learning to order his facts in making a survey and using his mind to draw conclusions from them. A student in casework may be going through much the same process in coming to assessment regarding an individual's problem. Are these tasks comparable? Are similar skills required? Discussion and review will provide the answers, and eventually a group can determine a significant number of comparable and measurable activities which may provide a basis for grading.

Whether the supervisor is concerned with comparatively fine measures of grading or the broad decision of pass or fail, the tasks remain to decide what must be measured, to assess the evidence, to come to a decision and to share that decision with the student. If the decision is that the student fails, the task is not a pleasant one. Few, if any, supervisors like to fail a student; yet if the student is really not up to standard, failed he must be. Fortunately the task is shared with the student's tutor, but the supervisor will have to face the student in an evaluation session with the fact that his work has not met the requirements. This should not, of course, come as a surprise to the student. He and the supervisor will have been discussing his inability to meet standards throughout the placement, but both may have been hoping he could somehow make it. When the final decision that the student has, in fact, not 'made it' must be faced, there may be little surprise; but it remains a difficult moment for both. It is far easier for the supervisor if the student realises for himself that social work is not for him. The task then may be to explore where his talents lie and encourage him to think of moves into new fields. It is those students who continue to want to be social workers who present the supervisor with his most difficult task. As long as agencies employ unqualified workers, they may have a chance of continued employment. Should they continue as unqualified workers? Can the supervisor help them to sort out what their limitations are and what elements of the social work job they are equipped to do?

Fortunately the failures are proportionately few. For most supervisors and students, evaluations provide an opportunity to confirm good work and plan developments for the future.

TERMINATION

'In the end is the beginning' is strongly applicable to student supervision, however one may interpret this somewhat ambiguous statement. As the placement ends, most students are looking forward to a new beginning, another placement or paid employment, where they may use the knowledge and skills they have acquired. At the same time, it will be apparent that how the student began the placement will affect how he ends it.

At the beginning much of the learning was focused on how to develop relationships; now the student must learn how to terminate them. Hopefully much will have been done earlier in the placement to help him with this task. As cases have been transferred to him, as he has succeeded others on assignments, he will have had the opportunity to see how these transfers have been handled. If from the beginning he has been encouraged to share with clients and others with whom he works the knowledge that his is a time-limited placement, the termination will have been to some degree anticipated. Some clients are particularly vulnerable in short-term relationships, children in residential homes, for instance. Where vulnerability is recognised, supervisors will have been helping their students to attempt to achieve suitable limits of 'controlled emotional involvement'. Yet when the time for termination comes, there is often a fair amount of emotional reaction on both sides. It is advisable for supervisors to make careful preparations for the final period and to offer teaching well in advance about the elements of transfer and termination.

Supervisory Tasks in Helping the Student to End His Assignments
Considerable thought and perception go into helping the student sort out the varying demands upon him as he moves towards terminating relationships with clients. In addition to whatever he and the supervisor may be discussing, many courses try to include material about transfer and termination in the academic work at an appropriate time before the end of the first field work placement. Often students will be referred to various articles which describe a range of the conscious and unconscious reactions that clients may display. The student may well be a bit over-whelmed at the import of all this. He learns of extreme client reactions; and, indeed, he should learn about them because some, at least, of his relationships may have been intensive and some, at least, of the clients may produce extreme reactions. Not all will, of course; and it is the supervisor's task to help him sort out what is applicable in various situations. An inexperienced student may well expect more reaction from his clients than is likely to occur. The situation is further complicated by his own feelings, often of guilt, at leaving the client. In some agencies where there is a frequent turnover of staff, supervisors are sometimes surprised at clients, thought to be inured to such changes, who react strongly to the loss of a student worker. They should remember that one of the factors affecting termination in student cases is that the student has often spent more time with the client than previous workers and may have invested rather more in the relationship, so that both client and student feel genuine regret at its break-up.

The supervisor will need to help the student to focus on handling the situation in ways that will be most constructive for the client. In this process they can look together at the various cases or assignments and assess what reactions may be reasonably anticipated. This helps the student to understand the part he has played in the past and is playing at the time of transfer and how this may affect the client's relationship with future workers.

In busy and often understaffed offices, it is not always possible to arrange joint transfer visits with the new worker; but it can be useful if the student is given this experience with at least one or two cases who may most benefit from such an arrangement. The supervisor should, when-ever possible, let the student know which workers may be taking on his cases so that he will be able to offer the client the tangible reassurance of a named individual who will be carrying on the service. One of the problems often facing student and supervisor at this time is the recognition that the new worker may not have as much time to give the client as the student has. The supervisor will need to help the student think out how he may best prepare his clients for a different approach so that they may make best use of what service is available. It is often useful to the student if he can have some time with the worker taking over so that they may discuss the transfer. This will give the student, toò, some idea of how the next worker sees himself in relation to the clients he is taking over. Realistically this can be either a comforting or a disquieting experience for the student, and the supervisor may find himself coping with some reactions. Nevertheless, it is better for the student to know. The worst possible situation for the student at this period is probably when, owing to staff shortages, his cases cannot be reassigned and are held for crisis work only in some sort of general pool. Most organisations in this situation do at least encourage students to assure clients that they may get in touch with the agency if and when they again feel the need for social work support.

In the last days of placement the student will be concluding his recording. It is important for him to learn the skill of writing concise, clear transfer and closing summaries, so this becomes one of the final teaching tasks of the supervisor. He will need to encourage the student to start recording in sufficient time for his reports to be reviewed to ensure that they meet the needs of the agency. As far as possible last-minute appointments that would require further reporting should be discouraged.

Supervisor's Tasks in Terminating the Student Placement

In addition to helping the student to terminate his assignments, the supervisor will find his own final days of the placement somewhat demanding. Students do and should go on learning right up to the end of the placement, but the goal is to achieve a balance between a too full and hectic termination and one that drags boringly to a close with time unfilled and wasted. As the placement draws to a close and final evaluations are in preparation, awareness of accomplishments and of gaps in the teaching/learning process is sharpened. Inevitably some things have not been covered that one or both had anticipated. Some few, perhaps, may still be included, but the supervisor will need to resist the temptation to try to cram too much into the final days. Some things will have to be left to the next placement or work experience. The rare student may have wound up all his transfers well ahead of time, in which case student and supervisor together will need to assess the remaining time and use it in ways that may be of interest or benefit to the student.

Perhaps there should be some consideration, too, of the feelings involved in terminating the student/supervisor relationship. It is not unknown for the student to react (rather like some clients) with either regression or a sudden spurt of learning. The supervisor may feel regret at the loss of a mutually satisfying relationship or relief at the end of a demanding task – or a mixture of both feelings. The supervisor needs to be aware of the reactions and feelings involved in termination and should focus on helping the student to a successful ending and another beginning.

At this point the student and supervisor are definitely terminating one kind of relationship. They may or may not see each other again. They may or may not turn out to be close working colleagues or friends in the future. They will not, however, again be brought together in the purposeful relationship of student and supervisor which they have maintained throughout the placement. If they have enjoyed the relationship there will be regret at its ending, but they will both be moving to new duties and new relationships. The supervisor who has given his student a positive experience in the use of supervision will have given him a useful base from which to continue his professional development.

CONCLUSIONS

In this chapter we have been discussing the process of evaluation that is necessary in any student placement. We have seen that it is a continuing process, punctuated by set times for formal evaluation which serve as assessment of work accomplished and provide guidelines for future learning and teaching. We have seen that there must be full participation by both student and supervisor. The supervisor's tasks will include preparation for formal evaluations, holding discussion sessions with the student, writing the evaluation, sharing the written evaluation with the student and making use of evaluations in subsequent teaching. The culmination of assessment is either a grade or the decision to pass or fail the student. As the placement draws to a close, the supervisor helps the student to understand not only the factors involved in terminating his assignments but also how his accomplishments in this placement relate to his future development as a social worker.

FURTHER READING

Eric Baker, 'Supervision and Assessment: Impossible and Inescapable', *Social Work Today*, vol. 6, no. 7 (1975).

D. W. Millard, 'The Examination of Students' Field Work', *Social Work Today*, vol. 3, no. 14 (1972).

G. Rankin, 'Personal View', *Social Work Today*, vol. 5, no. 8 (1974).

Harry Salmon, 'Evaluating and Assessing Community Work Students', in Catherine Briscoe and David Thomas (eds), *Community Work: Learning and Supervision*, George Allen & Unwin (1977).

Doreen Wilson, 'Supervision and Assessment: Education or Injustice?', *Social Work Today*, vol. 6, no. 7 (1975).

PART FOUR:
LEARNING AND TEACHING SUPERVISORY PRACTICE

Chapter 12

DEVELOPMENTS AND EXPERIMENTATION

The process of supervision is far too complex, the demands today on both staff and student supervisor are far too great, for trial and error methods to be a satisfactory way of learning to supervise. In the early days of the profession there was no formal training for supervision. A skilled practitioner would be selected for 'promotion' and become a supervisor, often successfully, but sometimes with disastrous results. The qualities sought were those most useful to the casework emphasis of those days. Sensitivity to clients and the ability to develop a therapeutic relationship were not always complemented by administrative and teaching skills. The sometimes inept attempt to translate skills from practice to supervision has left us to this day with a fear of 'caseworking the caseworker' and of the over-supervision that kept workers in a dependent role. To their eternal credit most of those 'promoted' did manage to learn what was necessary to become good supervisors. It is the results of their experiments, thinking and writing that have provided us today with the body of knowledge for more formal training.

This chapter will be devoted to discussing some of the ways of providing education and training for supervisors. The first section will discuss the structure and content of a variety of courses now offered in either student or staff supervision. The second section will contain proposals for field practice in supervisory methods and a report of an experiment in setting up a course with a component of supervised field practice in supervisory methods.

COURSES FOR SUPERVISORS

Courses in student supervision have been offered for a number of years. In Great Britain in the 1950s and 1960s the Home Office pioneered such courses and made them generally available to prospective student supervisors throughout the country in addition to those offered by course tutors to local supervisors. Courses for staff supervisors followed rather later, and now some professional courses have offered content in supervision to selected students.

Courses for Student Supervisors

Most social work courses today offer courses for new supervisors, and it should be possible for an intending student supervisor to take such a course either before he starts supervising or at least concurrently with his first student.

The content of such courses usually covers the major aspects of work with a student. Various sessions will focus on the initial phase, preparation for the student, planning, case selection, and so forth. There will be sessions on field teaching itself, perhaps discussion of some of the principles of teaching or how students learn. Almost invariably there will be a session or sessions on evaluation. In short, most of the topics covered in Part Three of this book will be introduced in such a course. In addition to lectures and reading references, most prospective supervisors find the small group discussions particularly helpful. Here is a chance to get questions answered, to exchange ideas. The supervisor may have the chance of some role play as well. Some people are reluctant to enter into role play, but it is an invaluable experience for new supervisors. It gives them a chance to try themselves out in a supervisory session before they take responsibility for introducing a student to the use of supervisory sessions as a way of working and learning together. In the author's experience, supervisors attending these courses are more willing to participate if all are engaged in the role play at the same time and without an audience. The participants are paired off and may simply scatter in couples to different parts of a large room to hold their supervisory sessions. They may be asked to begin a first session with a student or perhaps to imagine themselves in the middle of an evaluation session. Whatever the situation, they have a stated period of time in which to carry on. All self-consciousness seems to disappear as they become involved in the sessions. The noise level rises, but each pair is intent only on its own session, and it generally seems to come as a surprise when time is called. Later they will reverse roles in another session so that each has a chance to play both the supervisor and the student role. Much can be learned from each role and from the ensuing discussion. In addition, perhaps even more important, the new supervisor has had a touch of practice and may greet his first real student with just a bit more confidence.

Experienced student supervisors, too, frequently request further courses in supervision. These often take the form of workshops where the supervisors may meet together for discussion about various areas of interest to them. Sometimes they may concentrate on how to help students with certain characteristic problem areas in common (e.g. students moving directly from undergraduate work with previous experience, mature students with many years of experience, failing students). They may be interested in learning more about new methods being taught on the courses. A favourite topic at the time of writing is the implications for field teaching of the unified approach to social work methods. Some of this may well be covered in supervisors' meetings, but there is value in spending a longer period of time – a day's workshop, three- or five-day courses – during which supervisors can concentrate on developments affecting their teaching. Not only do such courses provide information and a chance to rethink one's practice in the area of student supervision, but they often provide the springboard for experimentation and research based in the field. The courses are usually sponsored by one of the educational institutions for which at least some of the participants may supervise. Sometimes it is definitely a workshop with the focus on the benefit to be gained from the exchange of ideas by experienced persons. Sometimes an outside expert is invited to present new ideas as a stimulus for further discussion and experimentation.

Courses in Staff Supervision

Courses in staff supervision were a later development than those in student supervision, and they are still not as widely available as is desirable. All too often a newly appointed supervisor or team leader must learn his job largely by trial and error, with what help he can get from a perhaps already overworked superior or colleagues in similar posts. Some courses are offered to team leaders already in post, but there is often confusion as to whether these are 'management' courses or courses in supervision which deal with both the administrative and the professional aspects of the post.

A course in supervision for team leaders should include clarification of the team leader's role, his lines of responsibility and accountability, equal emphasis on both management and teaching tasks, and discussion of his supportive and evaluative roles. These courses often provide a rare opportunity for team leaders from different area offices to get together and exchange ideas. Those offering such courses have frequently found that there was considerable confusion about the expectations of the team leaders or their expectations of themselves; hence the statement that such courses need to include (and early on) some clarification of the team leader's role. As with courses for experienced student supervisors, these courses, offered to practising team leaders, provide an opportunity for discussion which may lead to experimentation and research in some cases.

Few training sections seem to offer courses in supervision to experienced workers who may be expected at some time in the future to become team leaders. It should be possible to offer courses to those interested in preparing themselves for possible future assignment. A worker, learning about the elements of good supervision, could possibly become critical of his own team leader. However, experience with students learning about supervision tends to show that they become more aware and critically appreciative of the supervisor's tasks (see following sections).

Courses in Staff Supervision for Social Work Students

A few courses offering a professional qualification to students include content on supervision for selected students with considerable work experience. Criteria for selection for these classes vary, but they are usually limited to students who are already seniors or above or whose experience would qualify them for promotion soon after achieving their qualification. Such students may have had to expend energy and effort in adjusting to the role of students in field work, and it can be a considerable demand on them to bring their focus back to 'thinking as a supervisor' while they are still being supervised as a student in the field. In fairness to their student supervisors and to keep the focus on principles of staff supervision, it is usually desirable to set as a condition that their current experience of being supervised will not be used as illustration in the classroom discussions. The content of such seminars usually follows the topics discussed in Part Two, and the participants usually have sufficiently varied work experience to make their contributions and challenges mutually beneficial.

FIELD PRACTICE IN SUPERVISION

If, as has been postulated in this book, supervision may be considered a method of social work, field practice should be of value, as it is in other methods. The actual practice of supervision under the guidance of an experienced supervisor provides the prospective supervisor with the same opportunity to test theory in practice, to try out new methods and to develop skills as does the student placement in casework, group work, community organisation or residential work.

Such placements are not easy to arrange. Agencies will authorise students to act as workers accountable to their supervisor for fulfilling a worker's duties as a representative of the agency to both clients and others with whom they come in contact. They have more qualms about authorising a student to carry any authority in their administrative hierarchy. Perhaps an account of the setting up of a programme for field practice in supervision at the University of Newcastle-upon-Tyne will illustrate both the difficulties and the possibilities of providing such opportunities.

Establishing Placements in Supervisory Practice

The students for whom practice in supervision was sought were on a one-year course for mature students. All had had a minimum of five years' experience as social workers and were over thirty-five years of age. Each year about a quarter of the students came on the course from posts of team leader or above. Of the remaining students, at least two-thirds were expected to move to such posts shortly after obtaining their qualification.

A pilot project was undertaken with one supervisor and one student. The supervisor, a team leader, asked for volunteers from his team to work with the student and eventually selected a young, recently qualified worker who was having some difficulty with caseload management. The student had had no previous supervisory experience, but he had been an able worker for some years in a local authority social services department similar to the one in which he was now placed. He continued to carry a small but varied caseload in this placement, and some time was set aside for him to hold regular sessions with the worker. The worker and his team leader had decided together what cases he would bring to the student for discussion. In addition their sessions were to focus on helping the worker improve his caseload management. The student, in his own supervisory sessions with the team leader, discussed his work with cases and his quasi-supervisory work with the worker, and he consistently demonstrated that he was achieving considerable learning in both areas. At the end of the placement all three who were involved were asked to submit reports. All had found the experience highly satisfactory. The worker reported that he appreciated the opportunity for discussion of some of his cases in more detail than might otherwise have occurred, and had found their mutual thinking helpful. He had also found the help with caseload management most beneficial. The student thought that he had learned skills in supervision that would be useful in the future and had found the experience challenging but rewarding. The team leader agreed with the statements of the other two and reported that he himself had found the experiment stimulating. It had made him rethink some of his own practices, and he was most enthusiastic about continuing to develop this form of student supervision.

Concerns and Safeguards

On the basis of that pilot project, it was then proposed that several such placements should be offered to interested students in their final field work placement. Despite the enthusiastic report of the first supervisor, there were considerable reservations both in the supervisors' group attached to the course and in the social work community generally. The greatest concern was that this would take too much time away from the major focus of the placement (usually casework). The gist of the remarks most frequently made was that it seemed a shame for experienced students who had only one year away from the pressures of the job to be deprived of any time in which they could concentrate on casework. All agreed it was important that students coming on the course should be given full opportunity to develop their casework skills and understanding. Some thought they should devote full field work time to this; while others believed that if a sufficiently good standard of casework was achieved in first placement they might also add on some supervisory skills. Few at that time recognised that understanding of casework might be enriched during the supervisory practice. Eventually, consensus was reached that those supervisors and agencies willing to participate would go ahead, leaving the option to others to join in in the future if they wished.

In the event, the plan that was set up proposed that the student should have demonstrated a good standard of practice in his first placement. He would begin his second placement in the ordinary way with the assignment of a few cases. After an initial period, if he continued to demonstrate a good standard of practice he could be assigned some supervisory tasks instead of additional cases. This use of the initial period had the added advantage that it gave the student time to learn about the agency and its practices, knowledge very necessary to the undertaking of any supervisory functions.

Another concern was that such an assignment would be upsetting to staff within the agency and confusing to the student if he took on supervisory as well as student roles. Area directors were particularly concerned because team leaders would be required to act as student supervisors. Some saw the team leader post as purely managerial and hence inappropriate for student supervision. All recognised that team leaders were already so overworked that taking a student might be an impossible burden. Some team leaders, who had had no formal courses or training in supervision, were hesitant about what they could offer a student in this area.

The safeguards devised concentrated largely on full participation of all concerned in any decisions regarding the proposed placements. Team leaders were to discuss the proposals with their teams, explaining the purposes and exploring any difficulties. No team member was to be under any pressure to work with a student, but it was hoped that at least one or more would volunteer. It was made very clear that the student was to be placed with the team as a student, but that some of his activities would involve offering consultation or taking on delegated supervisory responsibilities as well as carrying cases. Because he was a student, he would be recording and discussing his varied activities with his supervisor, the team leader; it would need to be clear that this was understood by and acceptable to all involved. The team leader who undertook this type of supervision should also be a 'volunteer'. Like many a busy caseworker, he too should realise that he was taking on even further commitments of time and energy when he took on a student. The student would be having concurrent seminars on supervision to support his field practice, and the seminar leader would undertake not only to make the syllabus and teaching notes available to the supervisors but to have frequent discussions of content in supervisors' meetings.

Developments as the Project Progressed

Five combined casework/supervision placements were used in the first year, more in subsequent years. The first were all in local authority social services departments, as it was assumed that students would feel more comfortable and have more to give in a familiar setting. Later, placements were developed in various voluntary agencies, in medical social work departments and in the probation service. With each new agency, and indeed with each new local authority, an exploratory period preceded the placements, during which the concerns noted previously would again be brought up, but they were increasingly easily resolved as findings from the earlier placements became available.

The placements did not attempt to involve the student in the full range of supervisory tasks and duties, but a variety of tasks could be experienced depending on the interests and capabilities of the student and what the agency could offer. The range of experience offered went from a minimum of discussing supervisory practices with the student's supervisor to actual involvement in a variety of supervisory tasks for most of the time spent in placement.

Some students simply wished to learn something about supervision but not necessarily to practise. They enrolled in the seminars on supervision and were given placements with experienced supervisors who were willing to discuss questions of supervision as part of the teaching. In all other respects the placement followed traditional patterns of student practice. The student had some opportunity to test the theory in practice by bringing questions arising out of the seminars to his supervisor for comment and illustration from the supervisor's practice. Some students preferred to concentrate on their casework practice and use their supervisors in this fashion.

For most students some element of practice was involved; and for a few, supervisory practice was very nearly full time. In placements where the student actually engaged in supervisory tasks, one or a combination of several of the following assignments was arranged:

Consultation to one worker on a regular basis, usually on two to three specially selected cases.

Consultation to two workers of different backgrounds and qualifications. Usually, one was a new worker or case aid, the other a qualified worker of some experience.

Conducting an evaluation discussion with the workers supervised on the basis of the work done together.

Participation (with the student's team leader supervisor) in management meetings.

Taking responsibility for the induction of new workers, planning their programmes, supervising first cases etc.

Leading team meetings on a variety of subjects. (One student very ably conducted a discussion meeting on the use of supervision with the team to which she had been attached.)

Working with the team leader on assignment of cases to team members.

Conducting studies of unmet needs or special areas of service.

During the early years of the experiment, supervisors tried various methods of teaching. As would be anticipated with field placements so deliberately varied to individual students' needs and interests, there continued to be considerable variation in the teaching although some common problems were faced and worked out.

Expectations regarding recording have undergone change. When students were first asked to record their sessions with workers, they tended to record details about the cases discussed and the plans agreed about them. Supervisors, used to student recording referring to cases, tended to accept this and discuss with the student the implications of the case and the validity of his suggestions. Gradually there came recognition that interaction between student and worker needed to be recorded. Student recording needed to be related less to the case and more to the worker if his supervisory practice was to be discussed. A student has given his supervisor something to discuss if he records, 'I told her I had dealt with several cases like this. I did this because I wanted to establish my competence in this area. However, I went on to point out that each case had its own unique aspects, and I wondered how she thought of tackling this one.' Gradually there has evolved a demand for a process type of recording of the supervisory sessions which includes the student's thinking about his role as supervisor with the worker as well as his understanding of the case presented. Some supervisors have supplemented this type of recording with occasional or regular three-way sessions with supervisor, student and worker discussing the preceding session between student and worker.

Evaluation of the student's supervisory practice posed some problems. Originally there was some reluctance to evaluate, particularly to include an evaluation of the supervisory practice as part of the evidence for a grade. For the first two years the project was considered experimental, and it was not thought that a student should be 'put at risk' because of his participation. However, it was soon recognised that if this was an agreed part of the student's learning, his work in this area should be assessed as any other field work.

Writing the evaluation presented its own problems. Various formats were tried. Some supervisors used a descriptive account of tasks undertaken with some assessment following each task. Others made their comments under the headings provided in the usual outline. Still others added a separate section. In the end it was agreed to organise the remarks under the usual headings. This was done because for the most part the placements were a combination of casework practice and supervision, and it was thought that the student's overall field performance could be more readily perceived in this fashion. The course then used an evaluation outline with five major sections: administration, service to clients, recording, use of supervision and development as a professional person. It was found that an assessment of the student's supervisory practice could be fitted into these headings. How he performed the administrative elements of his supervisory tasks and his understanding of organisational relationships obviously belonged in the first section. The teaching and enabling skills he showed in helping workers to serve clients came in the second. His recording of significant factors in supervisory sessions was assessed separately from his case recording in the third. His skill in offering supervision as well as his use of his own supervisor came under scrutiny in the fourth. Finally, his development of professional judgement and application of values in his supervisory role seemed appropriate to the fifth section.

Some Results of a Study of Field Practice in Supervision

For the first three years of these placements questionnaires were sent to all participants. The answers would seem to indicate that such placements are not only feasible but have a valid place in field training. As reported, one of the greatest worries at the beginning of the project had been the fear that students would be unduly limited in their casework learning. Questions addressed to both supervisors and students asked if progress in casework had been affected by the placement. In every answer from both supervisors and students the reply was that casework knowledge had been enhanced. This, perhaps, should not have been surprising since consultation with workers on cases would involve the student in both thinking and teaching about casework principles and practice.

Other questions were aimed at assessing if supervisors and students would have chosen to participate had they known at the beginning what they presumably knew at the end of placement about what it involved. All students who had opted for actual supervisory practice affirmed that they would have done so. Of those who chose not to try the actual practice (although having the chance to do so), 50 per cent reported that they had been held back by uncertainty and rather wished they had. A majority of the supervisors replied that they had been uncertain, indeed threatened, at the start of the placement but had found it satisfactory and requested that further students be assigned to them for supervisory practice. Most of those reporting in this vein stated that after the first week or two they had ceased to feel threatened. Since the threat seemed to come from a fear that the student would be critical of their own supervisory practices, it is interesting that the vast majority of students reported that involvement in practice had made them more aware of the difficulties their supervisors faced and more appreciative of the skills involved.

Questionnaires filled out shortly after the placement is completed can give no valid answer as to how useful the learning may be in the future. All that can be said is that it was the impression of the experienced team leaders and tutors involved that the students had indeed learned some skills that could be of use to them if they undertook subsequent assignments as team leaders.

Indication for the Future

Most certainly the experience of students and supervisors at the University of Newcastle-upon-Tyne indicates that the practice of supervisory skills can be taught in the field. Other courses are also experimenting along these lines. Some of the post-qualification courses concentrate more on the field practice than the experiment reported here, and it is to be hoped that a variety of such placements will be developed.[1]

If these placements were useful to students on a course leading to a professional qualification, it seems there is some indication that comparable field practice might be developed in many in-service training programmes. It has already been suggested that training divisions could offer courses not only to team leaders already in post, but to those interested in preparing themselves for these positions. Workers taking training courses in supervision would find their training enriched if they could have some field practice as well. It may be that training officers could work out a programme of field practice, using current team leaders as supervisors. The trainee supervisor could be given responsibility for supervising a new member of the team or a case aide under the supervision of the team leader. Whether it is deemed better to use the worker's own team leader or someone else, perhaps another team leader or the area officer, the important thing is too choose a well qualified person. The staff member studying to gain skill as a supervisor needs really to be supervised in his practice, not left to learn by trial and error.

CONCLUSIONS

Supervision is a method of social work for which both knowledge and skill are necessary. Based on the trial and error experience of many supervisors in the past and the thinking and research that have followed, courses have been developed to provide the necessary knowledge and discuss the skill involved. Such courses can be supported by field practice in supervision where prospective supervisors may have an opportunity to develop their skills and test theories of supervision in practice. Further experimentation is needed in the area of providing learning opportunities in the practice of supervision. The job of a supervisor or team leader is a demanding one, the post is a crucial element in the administration of the social services, and those undertaking such responsibilities need all the support that purposeful training and clarification of expectations can give.

REFERENCE

1 Ilse Westheimer, *The Practice of Supervision in Social Work*, Ward Lock Educational (1977). For a report of some other students' practice in supervision see Chapter 6.

FURTHER READING

Marilyn Burchill, 'In-service Training – Mobilising Resources to Meet the Circumstances', *Social Work Today*, vol. 9, no. 8 (10 January 1978).
Rosemary Hull, 'In-service Training', *Social Work Today*, vol. 3, no. 8 (13 July 1977).

INDEX

DATE DUE

GAYLORD   PRINTED IN U.S.A